World Famous Personalities

GOODWILL'S

WORLD
FAMOUS
PERSONALITIES

Roopa Gosain

GOODWILL PUBLISHING HOUSE
B-9, Rattan Jyoti, 18 Rajendra Place
New Delhi - 110 008 (INDIA)

Published by:
GOODWILL PUBLISHING HOUSE
B-9, Rattan Jyoti, 18, Rajendra Place
New Delhi-110 008 (INDIA)
Phone: 5750801, 5755519
Fax: 5763428

Price Rs. 75/-

Printed at Kumar Offset Printers, Delhi-110031

Foreword

This book has been specially written for the lay reader who has no time to read the biographies of the great inspiring people of the world but would like to, at a glance get aquatinted with their lives. The personalities included in the book are a blend of the past and the recent present. Inspiring personalities from all walks of lives are presented with a view to uphold the reader's interest.

The articles tell tales of valour, pursuit, dedication and courage. They tell us spell binding sagas of lives that have triumphed over adversities and have made a success of their lives. The articles also provide an insight into the psychology of human beings at different times and in different ages. But the common underlying factor in all these personalities is a fierce desire to succeed.

The book truly is an unforgettable experience amongst unforgettable people and will make good inspirational, informative reading for school going children, teenagers and all the family.

Hope you enjoy reading it.

Roopa Gosain

Table of Contents

Alexander The Great

To conquer the world was not only his dream but a reality which this young Greek general called Alexander had almost achieved, when, at the age of 32 he suddenly died. Dynamic, enterprising this young hero was spurred on by an insatiable appetite to have the world at his feet. Standing little over five feet he possessed that unique blend of youth and wisdom that today puts him in an unchallenged position amongst the world's greatest generals.

As the son of King Philip of Macedonia, Alexander was the beneficiary of his father's military and political genius. This together with the unsurpassed tutoring of none other than

Aristotle himself, Alexander's formative years inculcated in him a love for knowledge and life. Be it botany, science, anatomy, history, literature morals or political science Alexander found answers to all possible questions under the able tutelage of his teacher. This has made Alexander the most well read conqueror of all times. Due to his sagacious insight into military strategy great and much envied generals like Hannibal, Ceaser, Napoleon studied him.

It was in 336 B.C. on losing his father that Alexander donned the mantle of responsibility of the new King. At first it was thought that his father's military might be able to outshine any of Alexander's military exploits. But the Macedonians never could have been more far from wrong. Alexander struck north, east, west and then south into Greek proper. Once having all of Greece under his command the young general started looking outwards.

Leading his army Alexander marched towards Asia. Alexander thought that it was time to punish the Persians for invading Greece 150 years ago. King Darius III the Persian King laughed when he heard about the valiant Alexander who lead an army of a mere 30,000 infantry and 5000 cavalry officers against his vast army of a million soldiers! But it was Alexander who was to have the last laugh. Using a planned intelligent maneuver Alexander let his center draw the main enemy attack upon itself. This led the enemy to concentrate fully on the center. Alexander taking advantage of this carried out a wild but disciplined cavalry charge on to the unsuspecting right wing of the enemy. He caught the enemy unawares and this lead to an unprecedented victory over Darius's army. Darius fled the battlefield. Darius was killed by Persians conspirators. He was found lying dead by the Macedonian soldiers. The dying king muttered some words of gratitude to Alexander for treating the royal captives with courtesy. Alexander in his characteristic manner covered the body of the dead king with his own royal mantle as a mark of respect.

Alexander's bravery did not in the least dampen his humane approach to things. His annexation of the other Greek city states was done with tolerance and the least loss of life. It was only the plunder of Thebes that saw the ruthless exploitation by the Alexandrine army, but here too the characteristic Alexanarian touch spared the House of Pindar, the great thebian poet. He venerated all knowledge. In another instance, after winning over Darius's army, Alexander in a drunken state is said to have gone along with the demand of the Greek soldiers to burn the palace of their enemy down. Alexander himself lead the parade throwing blazing torches at the building, only to retrace his steps once the spectacle of that magnificent fire had a sobering effect on him. He then tried to save all that he could. Today because of this spontaneous act of saving the monument the archeologists have found wonderful stone carvings nearly intact.

Alexander had started his journey for Asia with the sole aim of making slaves of the Persians. He had been taught to think that the Persians were second rate citizens and were fit to be subservient always. But on experiencing the might of the Persian army and on close contact with the Persian soldiers Alexander found the soldiers to be noble, cultured and with great dignity. He was impressed. As a goodwill gesture he chose 30,000 of the best Persian soldiers to train in the Macedonian art of military leadership. These troops were also trained in the Greek language. Alexander was not a slave to prejudice. He acknowledged rare qualities of bravery and camaraderie even in soldiers of the enemy camp and he did not forget to respect them. On capturing a state in India Alexander defeated the king of Indus called Porus. He took the defeated king captive and then asked him as to how he would like to be treated. To this Porus replied, "Like a king". Much impressed with Porus's sense of honour and self respect Alexander restored his territory to him as a protected state under Macedonian regime.

Even today Alexander's tales of valour can be an inspiration to any aspiring commander of troops . He always fought right beside his men and never deterred to face fierce attack. When still a boy, Alexander was the only one to master the famous horse Bucephalus when it was brought before his father King Philip. Where stalwart riders had failed Alexander simply turned the horse towards the sun so that he could no longer see the sun and be frightened by it's shadow. Alexander coaxed and tamed the untamable brute. Bucephalus from then on was Alexander's personal companion. When Bucephalus died in India, Alexander mourned his death as one would a true friend. He founded the city of Bucephalia in memory of his beloved charger.

In another instance while facing the high fortified walls of an Indian city it was this son of Macedonia who unhesitatingly climbed the walls and jumped right into the enemy camp. He was at once accosted by the enemy who lost no time in attacking him from all sides. Alexander fought courageously but soon collapsed when a meter long arrow pierced his chest. Seeing their general set a bold example the other Macedonian troops swarmed in. On finding their general badly wounded they took to the streets with vengeance, slaying all who came in their way. Though Alexander was badly wounded he refused to be carried back. It is recorded that, at this time he asked for a horse and mounted it. He rode a few paces saluting his army and dismounting he walked to the cheers of his men. Such was his strength and such was his commitment to his soldiers that they followed him wherever he went.

This leader of men was driven by a lust of adventure that never could be easily satisfied. An ancient biographer wrote:"He would always have searched beyond for something unknown. "At the age of 22 he was the master of Asia Minor and at the age of 30 he had mighty Persia under his thumb. Alexander had been taught that the world did not stretch beyond the

Hindu Kush mountains. But, to his delight and on reaching the land of the five rivers, today's Punjab state in India, he found his spirits soaring as unexplored virgin territory spread before him for miles and miles. At this point it Alexander's surveyors had recorded that they had marched 18,100 kilometers in eight years. Alexander valiantly fought across the four rivers but on reaching the fifth river his army generals refused to follow him. The harsh unrelenting monsoons of the Indian soil broke their spirits. So their King had to give up hopes of further conquests.

By the time that Alexander died he had conquered an empire that would be every general's envy. His empire stretched from today's Yugoslavia to India and included all parts of Bulgaria, Israel, Egypt, Libya, Iraq, Iran, Afganistan and the Soviet Union. His exploits have left an indelible mark on the history and the culture of the places he conquered. Traces of Greek culture and art were found in the stonecarvings as far as India. The Oriental rugs bear the design of Greek art and Greek classics had found their way into the folk tales of Central Persia.

The only incident that tarnishes Alexander's impeccable record as the people's general and a superb administrator is a foolhardy drunken instance. All the Macedonian soldiers were not as generous in respect their opponents as was Alexander. There rose a discontentment between the soldiers when they saw their leader doling lenient punishments to their prisoners of war and in many cases Alexander was downright kind. The Macedonians could not understand this liberal stance. It was on such an occasion at Samarcand that Cleitus debauched with wine taunted Alexander that it was not Alexander that won the wars but the Macedonian soldiers that fought and were victorious. He also reminded Alexander that it was Cleitus that saved his life when Alexander was attacked by the infantry soldiers of the Persian army. He hurled taunts with such exaggeration that Alexander who was worked up to a frenzy, struck him down with a spear. It was a mortal blow and Alexander was inconsolable and chided himself a murderer.

Alexander married the beautiful daughter of Oxyartes of Sogdian Rock. Her name was Roxanne. It was in this matrimonial alliance that Alexander saw much happiness. Alexander's end came in 326 BC. After a huge drinking party he went to bed suffering of fever which eventually took his life. As word spread amongst his troops they all came to pay their last respects to this driving force of their lives. As the troops filed passed Alexander he lay their acknowledging their salute with the blink of his eyes for, he was too weak for any other movement. In his last moments too, this grand general never once forgot to respect his valiant troops for their unflinching and steadfast devotion to him. Though it has been more than 2000 years since Alexander walked the earth his footprints on the sands of time have left a lasting impression. His legacy of courage and leadership will always hold an inspiration to many an aspiring young warrior for generations to come.

Walt Disney

It would be appropriate to say that the creator of the fantastic Disneyland was one of the most dreamy characters that history has ever recorded. Owing to the fertile imagination that so gripped this gangly man with this country boy figure lost in deep thought, we would today perhaps still be foreigners to this concept of a sprawling amusement park that attracts millions of tourists from all over the world. The Disneyland at Orlando in the United States is the fruit of this creative genius's persistent effort to realize an idea once it gripped his imagination. The very concept of an amusement park was thought of as preposterous and a definite failure by all those who heard about it. But, it was solely on conviction and hard work that Walt Disney has earned a place in the hearts of people across the globe.

One of the earliest recollections that Walt's brother Roy has of Walt is his fascination for animals and his love for drawing. Walt grew up in the mid western pararie farm in a small town of Marceline. Amongst the romantic setting of the apple orchards and the weeping willows, Walt sketched his first impressions. The first nickel that Walt ever earned was for a sketch he had made of a neighbour's horse. His fascination for animals never ebbed and with an extra fillip of his imagination he immortalized them into characters we come across everyday be it on TV or comic strips or a full length cartoon movie. Walt's Mickey Mouse is now a household name that children of all races and nationalities enduringly associate with.

Walt began his career by launching a cartoon series called Alice in Cartoonland. He was 21 and the project was financed on a loan of 500$ that he borrowed from his uncle. Both Walt and his brother were in this together. Roy at the camera and Walt doing the animations. They worked hard . The series flopped. But undettered, Walt started a new series called Oswald The Rabbit. Oswald did better but Walt was once again duped by the distributor, who, having bought the copyrights, took charge of the series himself. Not disheartened at all, Walt made a significant decision that was to affect the future coarse of things. He decided to go into business on his own. With characteristic enthusiasm he said to Roy, "We are going to start a new series. It's about a mouse and we'll own the mouse. " Mickey Mouse was born that year and he celebrates his 70th birthday this year. Mickey was Walt's first success. His matchless imagination and his uncanny ability to turn the ordinary into something wonderful was applauded by the audience. But it was only with Snow White that their was a definite windfall for Walt. Walt made several million dollars on this one.

One would expect that the money rolled in after this stupendous hit. But this was far from truth. Walt invested nearly all that he earned into building a studio and doing more cartoon features. Walt never spared any expense on improving his pictures. His bankers, bookeepers and lawyers often tried to put brakes on his unbridled imagination. Once an idea possessed him he went headlong into realizing it no matter what the cost. His brother on seeing him triggered with that special nerve would often say, "When I see you happy, that's when I get nervous. "But it was this desire to see perfection in everything that makes Walt Disney the unmatched creative genius of our times.

All through the World War II and the Depression of the thirties it was the extraordinary partnership of hardwork and invincible faith that kept Walt afloat. During the Depression when the studio was on the verge on closing down Walt gave his staff a raise! It was thought to be a crazy idea. But, it gave a big moral boost to all. Walt involved himself in everything. He had an exacting eye for details. Rarely anything escaped him. During one story conference on the Mickey Mouse Club TV Show the story man pointer in hand was outlining a sequence called how to ride a bicycle. "Now when you get your bicycle. . . . . ", he began. Walt at once said, "Change your bicycle to a bicycle. Remember every kid is not fortunate enough to have a bike of his own. " He was a perfectionist. Though he demanded perfection from his crew, he never could fire anyone. If someone did not suit a job he almost always tried to find another job for him in his own concern. WED(for Walt Disney) Enterprises at Glendale was his favourite place to absorb people who could not fit into other departments. This place eventually was to become the illustrious Disneyland that the world throngs to see today.

Walt Disney's success can be credited to four things. Hardwork, a panache for details, extaordinary imagination and some luck. At the studio he worked the hardest. Nothing ever escaped his perceptive eye. Very often on retrieving some discarded work of an animator from the waste paper basket,

Walt would invariably write a note for the animators saying "Let's not throw away the good stuff." "In the jugglery of creative work Walt Disney knew what "good stuff" meant. With an extra gag or a new angle the whole thing would suddenly come alive. His ability to give a graphic description of a story was so overwhelming that his nephew preferred a story telling session with Walt, rather than see the actual picture. On seeing Pinocchio, the new animated Walt Disney production that won acclaims all over, was infact a disappointment for his nephew. He is known to have said, "It didn't seem as exciting as when Uncle Walt told it. "So, it can be safely said that the only rival his productions ever faced was Walt Disney himself!.

The amazing success of Disneyland did not in the least change this man's simple way of life. He hated parties and his idea of good evening was a hamburger and chili at a little restaraunt. The only extravagance was a little miniature railroad that ran on the grounds of his house. His passion for railroads can be traced back to his boyhood days at Marceline when, his Uncle Mike an engineer would sound two long and one short whistle to wake up these boys so that they could take a closer look at the locomotives. Walt never lost his love of trains. Years later one of the first attractions at Disneyland was an old-fashioned train.

Work was his passion and he perused it faithfully. The money earned was ploughed right back from where it came. A friend once asked, "What do you do with all your money?". "I fertilize the field with it", was Walt's reply. This financial stability gave him an opportunity to develop other fantastic ideas. Millions of dollars was poured into making an alpine like valley high in the Sierra Mountains, called Mineral King. He donated land and money to the California Institute of Art which was worth millions and he started the Disney World and the City of Tomorrow in Florida.

Walt Disney's enthusiasm would have gone on endlessly had it not been for the fatal illness that suddenly seized him in the midst of this hectic activity. But his enthusiasm did not leave him even in his last hours. His brother Roy records that the night before he died, Walt was full of plans for the future. This infectious celebration of life, which was so characteristic of Walt Disney is what Disneyland is all about. Through his creations the future generations will continue to celebrate what he once described as "that precious, ageless something in every human being which makes us play with children's toys and laugh at silly things and sing in the bathtub and dream." And to children all over the world he will always be the one that actually brought fairyland into their lives!

Eleanor Roosevelt

It is not easy to describe in a few words the wonder of that wonderful lady called Eleanor Roosevelt. Apart from being the First Lady of the United States as wife of President Franklin Roosevelt, she was to many who were touched by her life, an icon of warmth and friendship. Her tall stately appearance bustling with energy soon came to be regarded with much affection just after a few days in the legendary White House.

The formality of the White House was something that she could not understand. In a characteristic manner Mrs. Roosevelt declared boldly, "I shall not toe the line". It was more than on one occasion that the breezy informality of Eleanor's style not only came to be talked of in the stiff inner paneling of the White House but soon it was accepted and appreciated as well. She was the people's friend. Approachable on all occasions Eleanor's spontaneity was what endeared her to all who came in contact with her.

On her first day at the White House a woman reporter who wanted to get in touch with the First Lady's secretary to obtain some information was surprised as her call was received directly by none other than the First Lady. The startled reporter protested that she did not want to trouble the First Lady, but Eleanor Roosevelt insisted on personally getting the information that she wanted. "You may call me anytime," she said. She tried to bridge the gap that inevitably comes between the electorate and the elected. The royalty of red tapism was her one great enemy. She endeavored at all costs to behave like an average American citizen. She shunned the pompous grandeur that comes from being the privileged class. At the Inaugural Buffet, the President waited his turn like everyone else to be served . She scandalized everyone when she insisted on operating the lift herself. "This just isn't done Mrs. Roosevelt, "protested the lift man. "It is now", came the reply.

Eleanor's down to earth attitude and her forthright approach made her a familiar figure in the lives of everyday people. She would often commute by taxis or the underground. Very often she walked. Her own security was her least concern. When the Secret Service offered her protection after her husband narrowly escaped a bid on his life, Eleanor's answer was typical. "Nobody's going to shoot me. I'm not that important. "Sticking to her guns she refused to be under any kind of protection and insisted on living her own life the way she had planned. On the insistence of the Secret Service she learnt to use a revolver that she invariably forgot to carry!

It was the little acts of kindness that were so much a part of Mrs. Roosevelt's personality that made her one of the most popular figures of her time. However busy her schedule she always found time for a little act of thoughtfulness that would brighten another's day. When one of the band of women reporters that were covering her activities fell ill and was absent, Mrs Roosevelt at once noticing her absence asked the reason. On learning the reason, she organized a vacation at the Roosevelt house at Campobello for the reporter and her family. Ruby Black the reporter and her family did take a vacation as guests of Roosevelt. Ruby returned to her job reinvigourated. In another instance, a small town teacher bringing a crippled boy to Washington asked Mrs. Roosevelt's advice as to what they must see in the capital. Responding to this Eleanor not only organized a special tour for the boy but she also put up the boy at the White House. Such was her generosity and it only increased as the years rolled on. The White House' Housekeeper Mrs. Henrietta Nesbitt once said, "I have never known a woman except Mrs. Roosevelt whose motives were always pure kindness.

Mrs. Roosevelt received a deluge of letters every day. Her secretaries helped her to answer the official ones but the personal ones she always insisted on answering herself. "I want people to write to me," she said. "I think it's important for people to feel that in the house where the government centers they have a friend". Emma Bugbee a newspaper correspondent who covered Mrs. Roosevelt's activities over the years remembers that when once on a holiday she (Emma) sent postcards to a 100 odd friends from Europe. It was only Mrs. Roosevelt who replied by mail. Her interest in the people was genuine and she never missed an opportunity to show that she cared. When Emma Bugbee completed 50 years as a reporter for the New York Herald Tribune, and the office gave her little surprise party, it was none other than the former first lady who breezing into the room and congratulated Emma like an old affectionate friend. She had a dozen important things to do but as always she had time enough to fit in a little act of kindness. Though not conventionally a good looker people were often surprised to find that she was more appealing in person than her photographs . The camera was unjust because it could never convey the soft colouring of her fair hair, her frank, alert eyes and her patient endearing personality.

Another aspect of her personality was her amazing energy. During her tenure at the White House she kept an exceptionally tight schedule. Waking up at dawn she went riding at 6 am, had breakfast at 7 and was busy at her desk by 7. 30 Am. addition to her formal duties as the first lady she wrote a column for a syndicated newspaper and articles for magazines. She was also part of a newspaper guild. She took voice lessons, spoke on the radio, lectured . All the money she earned in this way she gave to charity. Patiently she would pour over her mail late into the night. She had this inexhaustible drive about her that was simply incredible. After a hectic day of engagements which started at 6 in the morning and would officially end at 10 in the evening Eleanor Roosevelt would still be aiming to do a few hours of work. She was never tired. Often she would say, "I'm never tired except when I am bored".

As a wife too she was a definite support to her husband. Her understanding of the national and international issues of the hour was acute. Very often the President would involve her on a subject that he was immediately concerned with. He liked to get her opinion. It was always an intelligent one that helped sift and sort out his own views. Once he incited her so sharply on a thorny issue that she furiously contradicted his views with a dozen points. The next day she was thunderstruck to hear him blatantly quoting her remarks to the British Ambassador as his views.

The President gave a free hand to his wife in all that she did. Though her ideas often outraged people, Roosevelt did not try to restrain her. He would say, "Lady, this is a free country. Say what you think anyway the whole world knows that I can't control you. "But there were moments when the first lady tried to be discreet. Once when she had to pay an exceptionally large bill she sent a note to the president's secretary that read, "Missy, I know F. D. R. will have a fit. "Roosevelt happened to see the message when Miss Leehand, his secretary was out . When she rerturned, she found written across it: "Pay it. Have had the fit. F. D. R." The biggest blow came when President Roosevelt suddenly died in office. But life had more things on her agenda. President Truman on taking over, appointed Mrs. Roosevelt as a delegate to the first assembly of the United Nations, meeting in London in 1946. She soon proved herself to be a well informed and able debator. At the General Assembly in Paris 1948, after the Declaration of Human Rights, which she had shepherded for three years she received a standing ovation as she walked into the conference hall. It was a tribute to her outstanding work as peace promoter of the world. She held her post till 1952. During these years she did all she could to help people in distress. She received over 1000 letters everyday all asking for some kind of help. All the people who had no 'high' connections would always think of Mrs. Roosevelt. People knew that they won't be disappointed.

During her term in public life Mrs. Roosevelt had circled the globe three times. She had, to her many achievements an interview with Krushchev in Russia. She faced a communist mob in India and swam with Tito on his island. She had in her life time written millions of letters and traveled millions of miles. But this inexhaustible energy began to flag eventually. She developed anemia. She thought that she had picked up some rare kind of germ. Actually she was suffering from bone-marrow tuberculoises. On November 7 right after her 78th birthday she died.

She was laid to rest beside her husband in the rose garden at Hyde Park. There were people from all over the world who came to pay their last respects to this lady who had touched the lives of millions across the globe. She had won so many hearts simply by being humane and kind. Even after her death the memory of her gentle heart lives on in the lives of so many people. After her death a housewife received a cheque of 10 $. She was the daughter of a hitchhiker whom Mrs. Roosevelt had picked up once. He was out of a job at that time. She found him a job. The man was so taken in by her kindness that he resolved to name his daughter after her, if he ever had one. When a girl was born Mrs. Roosevelt asked to be the girl's godmother. The girl grew up and married. Each birthday she received a 10 dollar cheque from her godmother. The last came on November 10. It bore a feeble signature. It was posted a day before she died. "That was the kind of woman she was", the housewife said. "She never forgot".

Eleanor Roosevelt lived a full life. Her own words sum up her life the best. ". . . . I could not at any age be content to take my place by the fire side and simply look on. Life was meant to be lived. One must never turn his back on life." She never did.

Leonardo Da Vinci

The dawn of the Renaissance saw the birth of one whose name would be etched on the pages of history for generations to come. His name was Leonardo Da Vinci. He was a great painter, writer, scientist, a mechanical and civil engineer, mathematician and a natural philosopher, that the world would only come to revere after his death. Painting was the only field in which Leonardo's genius was acknowledged in his time. But here too he was not without competitors like Michaelangelo and Raphel.

Born on April 15, 1452 at Anchiano, Leonardo was born out of wedlock. His mother was Caterina, sixteen year old daughter of a peasant family. His father was Piero da Vinci a lawyer. As was the custom Piero da Vinci married another girl of a well known family, bought Leonardo from his mother and raised him as a legitimate son. Thus, the early years of Leonardo were spent on the family estate near Florence. Amongst the lovely countryside of parasol pines and winding streams, crags and wild flowers natures best made impressions on him that were to blossom into the breathtaking beauty of his landscape paintings. How often he must have gone back in his mind's eye to capture that freshness of pulsating nature that has now become synonymous with Leonardo's name. It was at the feet of mother nature that Leonardo seems to have found a substitute of a mother he was never allowed to meet.

For the first few years of his life Leonardo was an only child. He was thoroughly spoilt. But the startling combination of good looks and a quick wit made it impossible for anyone to wield the stick on him. It was this child of nature with music in his heart who captured the very essence of nature in his drawings. It was at this time that Piero da Vinci discovered his boy's gift for recreating the world on his canvas. He placed him as an apprentice in the studio of Verrocchio in Florence.

Leonardo grew up into a handsome man with an enviable combination of beauty and brains. Florence was the place where Leonardo's genius found an outlet and an audience. At Verrocchio's studio he met other artists like Boticelli. They became good friends Leonardo studied mathematics, physics, botany, anatomy, geography and astronomy not as essentially different to art but as a part of it. He saw no difference between art and science for both were different ways of describing God's universe. Often he would wander through the courts and churches of Florence studying the architecture of the place and the mingling of the different hues at different times of the day. He was an observer who studied his subject in detail. To clothe his naked canvass with the essence of beauty he would follow beautiful or grotesque people and study them.

He visited the hospitals to see the old men die and hastened to watch criminals hanged. The tenderness of motherhood as the baby suckled greedily at his mother's breast, the painfully contorted faces of soldiers dying, the serene beauty of a young woman kneeling in prayer are some of the many observations he took down on paper. He was a man who was in love with life and missed no opportunity to capture any impression of life however fleeting it might be.

Surprisingly, it was not as a painter that put him on the path of recognition but as lyre player . He was recommended by Lorenzo de' Medici, called The Magnificient, to Ludovico Sforza, called The Moor. Sforza was the tyrant behind the throne of Milan. It is here that the scientist in da Vinvi found an expression. On taking charge of his duties he realized that it was not only painting the cold, brutish face of the Sforza that was part of his charter of duties but also the instillation of pluming of the Duchess's bath. This transfer to The Moor's kingdom proved to be a blessing in disguise. It afforded opportunities to the young da Vinci that had never seemed possible. During his tenure at Milan he built an elaborate system of canals for the city and drew up plans never to be adopted, for two levels highways to handle different kinds of traffic. He also planned and executed fortification in the Alps . It was to be their defense against their invasion from the north. In military science he was indeed a genius. His note books prove that he could cast a cannon with thirty three barrels, of which eleven could be fired at a time. He designed and planned conical shells, grape, sharpnel, gas bombs and gas masks. He made time fuses, hand grenades, mounted his artillery on wheels, and invented a breech-loading gun to replace the clumsy muzzle-loaders.

Today it is known that Leonardo more than four centuries ago understood why birds take off into the wind and how the slotted wing helps them mount more steeply. He experimented with paper models and was the first person ever to hit upon the idea of a propeller for locomotion. He foresaw the machine and had sound theories but lacked the knowledge of a light engine imperative for such a flight. He was the first man to mount a magnetic needle on a horizontal axis. This gave us the compass. History has put him down as the inventor of a differential gear and a wind guage. It has been recorded that he planned large submarines but later destroyed the pans for he thought that there was too much wickedness in the hearts of men to entrust such a secret to them. He wanted to prevent the practice of assassination at the bottom of the seas. To Leonardo goes the credit of pioneering studies in geology. He understood the significance of fossils. Long before Galilio discovered the telescope Leonardo realized that the earth moved around the sun and that it was not the center of the universe as it was believed to be during his time. He had in his lifetime discovered that general configuration of the solar system as we know it today.

Most of da Vinci's discoveries would have remained unknown had it not been for the persistent effort of collectors all over the world who compiled and published all that could be retrieved. After da Vinci's death his notes became scattered and collectors valued them not for their invaluable findings but for their authors precious autograph. It is interesting to note that this multifaceted genius had an eccentric style of writing. He was to begin with left handed and later became ambidextrous. He also wrote right to left. So, to read what he wrote one had to hold it in front of the mirror.

One of the most astonishing records of this great mind was his familiarization with the atomic theory of matter. He wrote: "There shall come forth from beneath the ground that which by its terrific report shall stun all who are near it and cause men to drop dead at its breath, and it shall devastate cities and castles. It shall seem to men that they shall see new destruction in the sky, and flames descending there from".

Today Leonardo da Vinci holds a position in the annals of history as a supreme artist. His name is synonymous with great art. it was in the breathtaking Engadine, that he saw the smoky twirl of waterfall cascade through the rocks and born from therein the very freshness of nature. This impression fused with the boyhood remenencies brought to life his masterpiece the Virgin of the Rocks. Betwixt this sensational mingling of the flora and fauna the adorable Mother, the beautiful Angel, the Child curling baby fingers in blessing over his playmate St. John have been immortalized. This picture was bought by the King of France and hung in his palace at Louver in Paris. Leonardo had done a copy of the same painting . This is the one we find in London's National Gallery today.

The famous *The Last Supper* was painted by Leonardo on the walls of a convent's refractory. The plaster of the wall was unsuited for pigments and within twenty years the mildew and the flaking began disfiguring the painting. Later a door was cut into the wall and Napoleon's soldiers took great pleasure at taking pet shots at Christ and his Apostles. The painting was greatly damaged. Today what we have is the painstaking work of the restorers who after consulting the numerous sketches and drawings of Leonardo tried to recreate the original passion and essence of the work.

There are only a few paintings that Leonardo actually finished, though he sketched voluminously. It seems that he never considered any work well done or actually finished. This may be the reason he almost never signed his name.

Historical happening disrupted his peaceful existence in Milan. The French invasion drove the Sfrozas out of Milan. Leonardo escaped to Mantua, then to Venice, Rome and Florence. He finally came back to Milan only to find himself in a financial tight spot. The Moor had neglected to pay his salary. So da Vinci accepted odd jobs as an engineer and a free lance artist. It is at this point in his life that the famous Mona Lisa was produced. It is the portrait of Lisa Ghererdini, wife of Messier Giocondo of Florence. She wears severe black in the picture as a mark of mourning for a baby she had recently lost. She was twenty one when she started to sit for the portrait and when Leonardo finished six years had elapsed. Mona Lisa seems to be an embodiment of one of da Vinci's fantasies. In the painting she seems to be looking over your right shoulder and smiling. Leonardo considered it his masterpiece and never actually delivered the painting. He took it with him to France when King Francis I invited him to take up residence in France. The King bought the picture for twelve thousand francs and hung it in Louver.

Leonardo's last years were spent near Amboise in central France. At the age of fifty eight he looked quite an old man. From a self portrait done in 1510 an aged man with tired eyes looks on. The fatigue of packing up so much in one life time shows. Though one of the world's greatest prodigies Leonardo was at heart a lonely man . He probably never could meet another human being on his level. But nevertheless his agile mind must never have had a second's boredom. To the last, though his hands were paralyzed Leonardo always was brimming with some latest project that he had just conceived. His lively conversation, his courtly style and understanding smile gave him the charismatic status of a pop icon of today's world. People would gather for hours simply to get a glimpse of him.

On May 2, 1519 Leonardo da Vinci passed away. He lived in another age but to us today he still adorns the mantle of a master from whom we have yet a lot to learn.

Diana, Princess Of Wales

24 February 1981, in the white and gold ballroom of Buckingham Palace as the notes of the National Anthem died away the Lord Chamberlain came center stage and said that the Queen had commanded him to make a special announcement. Lord Maclean in a manner that befits royalty, announced, "It is with great pleasure that the Queen and the Duke of Edinburgh announce the bethroal of their beloved son, the Prince of Wales, to Lady Diana Spencer, daughter of Earl Spencer and the Honourable Mrs. Shand-Kydd". This was indeed an illustrious moment in the history of the British royalty as Lady Diana was chosen by the exclusive royal family of Britain to be the future Queen of England.

On 29 July 1981 midst the pomp, glamour and much glitterati Lady Diana walked down the aisle of St. Paul's Cathedral with Prince Charles, the heir apparent to the British throne. Lady Diana became Her Royal Highness the Princess of Wales. It was a fairy tale wedding that struck the very picture of romance. The world applauded and cheered as the starry eyed nineteen year old princess with a warm style and stunning looks waved to them as her royal carriage passed the heavily packed London streets. She was an instant success.

Diana was the third daughter of 8th Earl . He held a position as Viscount Althrop, King George VI's equerry between 1950 and 1952, and equerry to the Queen for two years after her accession in 1952. It was in 1954 he married the Honourable Frances Ruth Burke Roche, the younger daughter of the 4th Baron Fermoy. Diana was the couple's third daughter. She was born at Park House, in a rambling Victorian mansion, in the grounds of the Sandringham Estate, the Royal Family's house. It was only till the age of seven that Diana enjoyed a happy childhood. Matrimonial strife between her parents ended in a divorce at this time. She was then sent to a boarding school. In 1975 on the death of her grandfather her father inherited the title and became the 8th Earl Spencer. They moved to Althrop, in Northamptonshire. Diana became 'Lady' Diana. Two years later her father remarried and Diana went off to a finishing school in Switzerland. She felt homesick and was back before the year was over. It was in 1977 at a shooting party that she met Prince Charles for the first time. Little did they know that destiny had more plans for them than was afforded by this casual meeting. It was two after this that Prince Charles started taking more than a casual interest in this unaffected 18 year old girl. She was a marked contrast to the more worldly girls in his circles.

At first their marriage seemed happy enough. Within a span of three years Diana gave birth to two sons, Prince

William of Wales and Prince Andrew. The four of them presented a picture of a happy family. Princess Diana had all that the future Queen of England must possess. She became an obsession with the media. Her gorgeous good looks with a model figure matched by a warm elegance became a perfect story for the print world across the globe. She was always in the news, sometimes as 'Shy Di', sometimes as 'Disco Di' and other times as 'Caring Di' or 'Crusading Di'. So powerful was her appeal with the masses that many a time her charisma and charm overshadowed the more sober Prince Charles. Her fanfare was phenomenal and she gained a tremendous amount of applause when she associated herself with unfashionable and controversial issues like leprosy and AIDS. She soon gained the stature of a model lady of the 20th century. She became an icon.

Unfortunately this idyllic state did not last . Hints of a strenuous relations between the couple became apparent . In December 1990 separation of the royal couple was announced by the Prime Minister in the House of Commons and in 1996 they were divorced. Diana's title of Her Royal Highness was taken away and she came to addressed as merely Diana Princess of Wales. This move by the royal household earned them a poor reputation as the world opinion was with their very own Diana. In a candid BBC interview she said that what she wanted most was to be not the Queen of England but the Queen of People's Heart's. And that she definitely was.

It would indeed be difficult to delineate the causes of the failure of this marriage which started with so much of hope and optimism. The formality of the monarchy which Diana found stifling together with the hounding media are surmised to be two major causes of the breakup of this marriage of the century. Prince Charles tutored to keep the proverbial tight upper lip could not perhaps understand the spontaneousness of the girl he had married. They were two kind but different type of people tied together in a set of circumstances made painful by fate.

The divorce could not rob Diana of the charm that she was endowed with. Her popularity never flagged, though there were articles every now and then about some clandestine romance that she was supposed to be having . But all was quelled when Prince Charles too confessed of having a relationship with his companion of many years, Camilla Parker-Bowles the public opinion as always was on her side. To the public she was a lone brave mother of the royal household trying desperately to bring the much needed contemporaries into the portals of the British monarchy. The people identified and sympathized with her.

Though no longer the wife of the heir apparent to the British Throne Diana had a significant role to play as the mother of the future heirs of the country. She decided to forge a new bond with the public that gave her so much adulation. She focused on causes that needed her attention. Her association with the AIDS trust, Leporsy Mission, cancer hospitals and the British Red Cross won her many laurels. She was a symbol of refreshing New Royalty that even shied away from wearing gloves when shaking hands!

Thus when on 30 August 1997 when the world heard of Diana's death in a car crash at Paris there was gloom that spread in all the corners of the world. There was a common outpouring of grief as people participated in what seemed a global loss. It was history in the making. They all mourned the snatching away of a one so young and irreplacable. Ironically it was on this fateful day that Diana had truly found personal happiness. That evening her companion and friend Dodi al-Fayed, the eldest son of Harrods owner had presented Diana with a fabulous diamond studded ring that commemorated the start of a new life together. Diana put it on the third finger of her right hand. She had been on the threshold of a new life when both Dodi and she were killed in the car crash at Paris.

Diana's tragic death put an end to an era that had just started to take shape. It reinforced the finality of death and the contrasting elusiveness of life. People from all over thronged to the iron gates of the Kingston Palace, the official residence of the Princess and paid their heartfelt tribute in flowers and messages. Even 45 condolence books were a measure less for recording the monumental grief of these people who mourned her death as one does a close friend.

In her death Diana has been canonized with all the people who in their short but meaningful lives have left an unquenchable void. Diana's close friend and famous singer Elton John's first line of his song "A Candle in the Wind" poignantly captures the essence of Diana's impact on the world when bidding farewell he says, "Goodbye England's Rose." With the death of Diana a contemporary icon faded away but from these ashes was a legend of a Princess that will live on. . . . .

Harry Houdini

Imagine if a man was tied and locked in a packing case that was bound with steel tape and dropped into the harbour off the Battery in New York City. What does one suppose would happen to such a man. Surely, he would meet his end. But this is exactly what did not happen to Harry Houdini the famous magician of the late nineteen and early twentieth century. He emerged free on the water surface within sixty seconds. Houdini was the man no lock could hold.

Houdini was born in 1874 in Budapest, Hungary. He was the fifth of the eight children of a poor Rabbi. His Jewish name was Ehrich Weiss. His family migrated to the United States when Houdini was still an infant. They settled in Appleton, Wisconsin. To contribute to his family Houdini worked as a newspaper boy and as a shoeshine boy. Houdini's fascination with locks started early. It was in a luggage shop that he worked in that Houdini discovered this. When he was 16 years old on reading the autobiography of the famous French magician Jean Eugene Robert-Houdin, Ehrich decided to be a magician. Modifying the surname of the great man Erich Weiss came professionally to be called Houdini. He started his career in 1882 as a trapeze performer. This lead him to later achieve astounding feats in the world of magic. He could extricate himself from any kind of shackles that anyone chose to impose on him. Handcuffs, ropes, locked trunks of any sort were no hindrance to him. When still a boy of 17, Houdini took to performing his art in front of any audience he could get. He did this on a part time basis. For during the day he worked as an apprentice cutter in a tie factory, only the evenings afforded him time to perform. Whenever someone would hire him for an evening or a week end show Houdini would put up a spectacular show . A quick switch trunk escape was one of his favourite performances.

Surprisingly, in the early years New York still had not acknowledged this great man's art. Dissillusioned with the lack of response he set out to London to make a mark. But on reaching the famous Alabama Theater in London, Houdini was unable to impress the manager with his portfolio of tricks. The manager mocking the young magician asked him to go down to Scotland Yard and "if", he said, "you can get out of their handcuffs I might give you a try." It was the famous Scotland Yard that really was responsible of putting Houdini on the road to success. At "The Yard", Houdini persuaded a young superintendent to handcuff him. Houdini was likewise handcuffed to a pillar. The superintendent then in a jocular fashion said that he would come to free him only after lunch. To the astonishment of the policeman Houdini replied "Wait a second. I'll go with you!"Saying this he handed the handcuff to the stupefied policeman. Houdini became an instant rage . All of England acknowledged his talent. He was the man whom no lock, no fetter, no restraint could hold. By 1905 he was a celebrity in Europe and America.

Houdini was a short man of about 1. 65 meters in height. Not a great conversationalist, on meeting him one would hardly think that he would be able to capture for hours the attention of a mesmerized audience. His incorrect diction and far from perfect use of the language made him the most unlikely candidate for a performing art. But only on adorning the magician's mantle did he turn into the most spectacular showman the world had ever seen. On stage he underwent a complete metamorphisis. Robust and confident, his speech became every orator's envy and sitting in front was the most enchanted audience.

Houdini's mastery of craft was outstanding. But through out his life he maintained that magic was nothing but a set of tricks that could be scientifically proven. On psychological principles of misdirection, suggestion, imitation and concealment the magician's victory is based. Sleight of hand, that is deception of manual dexterity is one of the methods that magicians use to outwit the audience. Mechanical methods involving the use of camouflaged apparatus that the audience sees but does not comprehend and of apparatus that is not seen are some of the jugglery secrets that the magician's use to perfection. Houdini practiced this art with utter seriousness. He improved many folds on the art of his Egyptian ancestor Dedi who is recorded to be the first magician in the history of mankind. He flourished in 2700BC.

Between 1895 and 1926 Houdini was a phenomenon. An escape artist, a magician, inventor, filmstar, aviator, showman and an author of more than 40 books, Houdini's was a sensational story. In Moscow on one occasion he challenged Moscow's secret police chief that he could free himself from

The Caret-a two meter square, steel-sheathedcube that was used to transport dangerous criminals to Siberia. It had only two openings-a tiny 20 centimeter barred window and a steel door. This door once locked could only be opened by a second key kept by the Prison governor in Siberia, 3000 kilometers away. Houdini was stripped naked and checked thoroughly for any concealed tools or pins of any kind. He was then chained and handcuffed. The great steel door was vaulted and The Caret was moved against the wall of the prison so that the door of the vault was against the prison wall. The Moscow Police left no stone unturned to ensure a fool proof vault that could now only be opened in Siberia. With Houdini locked inside they were satisfied only to be completely thrown off balance when they saw a sweaty Houdini emerging from behind the cell. The seal of the door was still intact. The chains that held Houdini were also locked. But Houdini was free!How he managed to do this still remains a mystery.

During his lifetime Houdini was a subject of much debate and speculation. Sir Arthur Conan Doyle, the creator of Sherlock Homes accused him of having supernatural powers. A German reporter once wrote of him that Houdini had the ability to de-materialize his body and pass it through the walls. At the Washington federal penitentiary Houdini escaped from a maximum security cell and also moved 18 other prisoners into different cells in 27 minutes. As always Houdini claimed that all could be explained scientifically. In an interesting instance he once set out to demolition a yogi's claim to supernatural powers that enabled him to be buried alive. After a lot of practice to stay without food Houdini climbed into a coffin, with hands on his breast and allowed himself to be sealed inside with the limited amount of oxygen. After an hour and a half on his release he told the reporters that this too was just a trick. By training himself not to eat or drink 24 hours beforehand and by remaining still he trains himself to use less of oxygen, so he can survive. This was the excruciating length into which that

Houdini could go to train himself. Behind the story of his success is the secret of a lot of hardwork.

The last years of Houdini's life were devoted to relentless campaign against fraudulent mediums. His thorough knowledge of deceptive techniques enabled him to expose them. Houdini challenged Margery the Boston queen of mediums. Her act guaranteed a direct contact with the world of beyond. The Scientific American was ready to pay her 25004 for a genuine contact with the other world. Houdini hearing this took up the challenge of exposing her. He was ready to pay 10, 000$ to anyone who could convincingly put him in touch with the world of spirits. He was sure that his art of necromancy could duplicate any trick that Margery could play. Cancelling his scheduled performance he traveled to Boston with the aim of breaking the Margery myth. His only condition was that he be allowed to sit next to Margery during the session. Before going for the session he desensitized his leg that was to be pressed against Margery's leg during the session. This would lead to exposure of her trick. As Houdini expected Margery at an opportune moment during the session made an almost imperceptible gesture to press a button with her leg. The movement was at once caught by Houdini whose leg extremely tender due to his intelligent tying of a band below his knee. Houdini caught Margery red handed. He proclaimed Margery a fraud!

The last years of Houdini's life were spent in debunking the myth of the 'Great Beyond' perpetuated by mediums all over the world. At the age of 50 he was at the peak of his popularity. But ironically it was at this time that the premonition of death began haunting Houdini. He knew his time was up. Just before setting out on a tour to Montreal, Houdini rang up the famous magician John Dunningner requested him on a rainy night in October 1926 to help him cart some boxes to a storage place at the other end of the city. As they were driving away, Houdini asked Dunningner to turn back. Houdini then got out of the car in the rain and stood before the house in silence for a few seconds. Then getting back in the car he said, "I just wanted one last look. I'll never see it alive again. "After an exhaustive tour at Montreal on the day of his last performing as Houdini was resting in his dressing room a group of young boys came to see him. They were very much intrigued by Houdini's confident denouncing the working of any of any kind of spiritual medium. One of the boys was infuriated at Houdini's rigid stance and without a warning punched Houdini in the stomach several times. The youth wanted to puncture the myth that Houdini was invincible and that the reality was that he could be hurt. Houdini was badly wounded and after a few days was admitted in the hospital for appendix and peritonitis. He died a few days later.

As in life, he remained a icon even after his death. Fake spiritualists taking advantage of his popularity began proclaiming that Houdini had contacted them and was sending messages to the world. It became a joke when the American wit Will Rogers said, "If Houdini keeps this message stuffup, he's going to put the Western Union (a telegraph company) out of business."

Today too, Houdini's grave is visited by earnest magicians year after year in the hope that the mystery man whom no lock could hold would send them some formula to make that greatest escape from the very clutches of Death.

Anne Frank

It was August 1944. The World War II was at it's height . Germany under Hitler's dictatorship was a menace . The Jews were being persecuted by the Nazis. The terror of fascism had spread. The Jews were desperate for survival. In a small office building in Amsterdam hiding from the German gun was the Frank family. Their only crime was, that they were Jews.

Anne Frank was the second daughter of Otto Frank a banker by profession. She was born on 12th June 1929. Her elder sister was Margot. They lived in Germany, till the unjust regime of Hitler's army made it impossible for them to survive. They shifted to Amsterdam in the hope of a life, free from Hitler's hatred. But this was not to be. In 1942 the family went into hiding. They lived in hiding for two and a half years. It was in this "Secret Annexe" that Anne Frank a young girl of 13 years recorded her daily life and impressions in a diary that she had received as a birthday gift. She had hoped to publish it after the war. The young girl had planned to see a brighter tomorrow, when the scars of hatred would only be a dim memory. But destiny had different plans.

On 4 August 1944 two Dutch Nazi soldiers and one German Nazi soldier stormed into the Secret Annexe and arrested the Frank family. Mr Kraler their Dutch friend and confidante, after being mercilessly harassed by the Nazi troops revealed the whereabouts of the Frank family. The Nazi soldiers arrested the Frank family and ransacked the place for money and jewels. In their endeavour for more booty they emptied Mr. Frank's briefcase. Anne's diary was in the pile of papers that was emptied on the floor. No one took notice of it then. A week later after the arrest, Miep, the Frank family's Dutch friend came back to the "Secret Annexe". She discovered Anne's diary. The diary contained all detailed information of the Frank family's life in hiding. It included help rendered by their friends like Miep, Elli, Mr. Koophius, Mr. Vossen and Mr. Kraler. It had volatile information. Miep risking her life kept the diary with her.

It was only in 1945 when Otto Frank by some weird stroke of destiny, surviving the horror of the concentration camp at Auschwitz, returned to Amsterdam. On reaching Amsterdam he learnt from a friend that his wife and daughters had perished. A friend described Anne's last days at Belsen camp as "cold and hungry, her head shaved and skeleton like form draped in a coarse, shapeless, striped garb of the concentration camp. "This description choked Otto with immeasurable grief. The image of Anne as his 'tender one' came to his eyes. Anne had been an overflowing bundle of energy. With her delightful chatter she had been a constant source of joy to Otto Frank. He could easily recollect, the delight that Anne had demanded from life. Her cheerful optimism in the face of the most demanding perils was a quality that few could boast of. Otto remembered Anne's boundless energy on their first day in hiding . The "Secret Annexe" had been in an unused state for a very long time. It was covered with cobwebs and dirt. Anne was, Otto remembered, not at all deterred. Instead she had plunged into the task at hand. Cleaning the shelves, dusting the cupboards and pasting pictures of her favourite film stars was done with characteristic enthusiasm. Otto could not believe that this little girl, with so much zest for life had now become a part of nameless history. His remorse was great when he realized that the past would now remain merely a recollection of fragments that could only be reconstructed again and again in the the long lonely hours of twilight. The horrors of the German genocide would simply become a distasteful part of human history, that would at best be recorded in some cold pages of a history book. The unforgivable German atrocities would only remain cold facts that happened to someone at sometime. For the future generations, the German holocaust would just be something they would like to forget.

It was at this juncture that Otto Frank met Miep the Dutch typist who had been the family's angel of mercy during their trying days in hiding. Miep gave Otto, Anne's diary that she had found in the "Secret Annexe". Seeing Anne's familiar writing scrawled across the pages overwhelmed Otto. It was days before he was able to actually get down to reading the diary.

Sensitively written the diary was an account of a girl's blossoming into teen age life. The pressures of a life in hiding were visibly marked in the words that she wrote on every page. After being isolated from the world for nearly 16 months Anne wrote, "I feel like a song bird whose wings have been brutally torn out and who is flying in utter darkness against the the bars of its own cage". The problems of coping with the unanswered questions of life were all portrayed with vivid clarity and depth. Beneath the veneer of a cheerful chatterbox was a girl with the most passionate heart and a profound insight into life that was almost ascetic. On religion she wrote, "People who have religion should be glad, for not everyone has the gift in believing in heavenly things."

Otto Frank was painfully torn by the past, that was gone forever. Reading the diary he rediscovered the person that was behind the the sprightly little girl. His daughter's attempt to conceal her inner fear and uncertainty so as to save her family from undue anxiety could only be categorized as brave. Her extreme love for her father, her inevitable adolescent conflict with her mother, together with the sibling rivalry between the two sisters documented in all sincerity made Otto Frank understand Anne even more intimately. It was this mass appeal that made Anne Frank's diary such a success all over the world. For generations now young girls who have read the diary have identified with Anne. After its publication Otto Frank was overwhelmed with the response he received from all over the world. A typical letter read, "Oh Mr. Frank, she is so much like me that sometimes I do not know where myself begins and Anne Frank ends".

At first Otto had no intention of publishing the book. He started to copy parts of the manuscript for his old mother who was still alive. He gave one typed copy to a close friend who inturn lent it to a professor of modern history. The professor devoted an entire article to it in the Dutch newspaper. The article was widely read. On popular demand Otto half heartedly gave the manuscript to Dutch some publishers, two of whom refused publication. The third publisher accepted it. It was an instant success. He sold 150, 000 copies of the Dutch edition alone. Other editions followed. The figure of the sale was phenomenal. Otto received letters from all over the world. Some were just addressed to, "Otto Frank, the father of Anne

Frank. Amsterdam. "The response was global. Otto had to retire from his business and take up the care of his daughter's book as a full time job. He answered each of the letters he received personally. All the royalties of the book were devoted to humanitarian causes. Otto felt that this is what his daughter would have wanted.

Anne Frank's life though short touched people all over the world. The dramatization of the book by Francis Goodrich and Albert Hackett, won the Pulitzer Prize for Drama in 1956-57. It played in 20 different countries to two million people. It ran in London for six months at the Phoenix Theatre. Twentieth Century Fox turned it into a film. The diary of Anne Frank written by an impressionable 15 year old girl in such candid simplicity, captured the hearts of millions all over the world. Anne's story retold in dramatic artistic mediums turned the cold facts of history into pulsating reality. Audiences when confronted with the thumping of Nazi boots on the stage were at once faced with their own failure as human beings. The onus lay, not on the Germans alone, but, on the whole human race for being nothing more than helpless spectators. The audience while seeing the play in heavy remorseful silence were afraid to face each other. Each one felt the burden of guilt. The Dusseldorf, producer of Anne Frank the play in Germany, talking of the success of Anne Frank said, "Anne Frank has succeeded because it enables the audience to come to grips with history, personally and without denunciation. We watch it as an indictment, in the most humble pitiful terms, of inhumanity to fellow men. No one accuses us as Germans. We accuse ourselves. "The drama strove to portray the futility of Anne's death and above all the futility of hatred itself.

Anne's life was an embodiment of faith in humanity. Midst such perils and racial prejudice Anne never abandoned hope in humanity. Despite harsh rejections Anne continued to trust. A passage in Anne's journal reads, "In spite of everything I still believe that people are really good at heart. "At Auschiwitz she proved to be a courageous leader. She dared to stand up for her rights and ask for food. Having lost her mother on their way to Auschwitz in a cattle-truck and being forced to separate from her father, Anne gained strength only from her sister's presence. Margot became Anne's reason for living this life of painful hardship inside the iron gates of Auschwitz where it was ironically inscribed "Work makes men free." Soon they were deported to Belsen camp where due to the unhygenic conditions of living, both the sisters caught typhus. They, nevertheless struggled on until one day, Margot lying above Anne's bunk bed suddenly collapsed due to fatigue. Margot's death snapped Anne's last tenuous link to life. It broke her spirit. Anne died in March 1945, two months before Holland was free and three months before her sixteenth birthday.

Anne's life healed scars that even a veteran psychologist would have found a daunting task. It instilled in the Germans a sense of shame and a desire to make amends for the past wrongs. German school children would often write to Otto Frank voicing their opinion against racial persecution. Any social home for young people, organizations combating Anti-Semitism or any other champions of human rights in Germany after the war all bore Anne Frank's name. Her name had become a symbol of secular and religious tolerance. Headmistress of one of the largest schools in England wrote to Otto Frank, "It must be a source of deep joy to you in your sorrow to know that Anne's brief life is in the deepest sense only just begining". In 1957 a group of 120 students cycled to Belsen to lay wreaths of flowers on the graves there. For one unnamed grave in the hundreds there, spoke a story of complete courage and faith in humanity. It had to be honoured.

Though gone forever Anne Frank has left behind a legacy of courage, faith and love for the future generations to benefit from. Anne wrote, "I want to go on living after my death. And therefore I am grateful to God for giving me this gift. . . of expressing all that is in me."

Imran Khan

Former captain of Pakistan's cricket team and an excellent player Imran Khan wields a celebrity status around the world. His consistently good performance in the field together with his outstanding good looks has endowed him with charm that has become legendary.

Imran Khan was born in Lahore on 25th November, 1953. He belongs to a rich family. He had his early education in Lahore and then was sent to England for further studies.

Khan made his test debut for Pakistan in 1971. After this he returned to Worcester Grammar school. He went up to Oxford in 1973 and captained the side the following year. In the field he displayed his all round skills as an outstanding batsman, bowler and fielder. At first he played for Worcestershire and then for Sussex. This 'Lion of Lahore' later led the the Pakistani team to many a success in the Test and the World Cup matches. It was in 1992, before retiring that Khan led his team to victory in the World Cup against England.

Throughout his career he maintained a debonair lifestyle. His handsome rugged looks were the camera's delight and Khan was always in the news. His popularity in the international circles was immense.

Post retirement Khan decided to stand for public office in Pakistan. His was a crusade against corruption which he felt had infested all crevices of Pakistani life. He headed a party called Tehriq-e-Insaaf. Though the party did not win any seat in the elections the spirit of the party was praise worthy. As Khan later said, "Tehriq-e-Insaaf was the first party in Pakistan to start talking about the VIP culture, this curse where human beings are treated unequally. "Khan's failure in this new venture has been accredited by many to his lack of political experience. By many journalists all around the world Imran was heralded as the ". . . first politician in Pakistan who has raised his voice against corruption. . . . . Imran's emergence in politics has run a chill through our corrupt elitist system".

The death of Imran's mother Shaukat Khanum in 1985 from liver cancer moved Khan to build the 550 million rupee, 250-bed Shaukat Khanum Memorial Cancer Hospital in Lahore. The hospital has a magnificent building and the latest equipment with the most well qualified team of doctors. In a barnstorming 30 day tour he raised 11.5 million rupees in 45 days. More than 300,000 Pakistanis have contributed to this laudable venture.

The first phase of the hospital was inaugurated in 1994 by a 10 year old cancer patient, Sumaira. This humane gesture characteristically embodies the spirit of the hospital. Reitterating the same spirit Mr. Khan said "There will be no VIP room or car parking in the hospital and the poor will be given free treatment. It is criminal to ask the poor to pay. "This charitable work has gained Imran khan the respect and goodwill that he deserves. A day after the inauguration an estimated 100,000 crowd at an entertainment function greeted the criketer turned social worker by waving national flags and shouting "Wazir-e-Azam Imran Khan" (Prime Minister Imran Khan).

To build a mass campaign for raising the literacy level in Pakistan and cleaning the environment are somethings Khan associates himself closely with. "If the government cannot do this, which I don't think any of these governments can, looking at the past record, then private individuals must come forward," Mr Khan has said displaying a sense of purpose and commitment.

Shedding his playboy image of his cricketing days Imran khan married Jemima Goldsmith, the 21 year old daughter of a Jewish tycoon in a Muslim ceremony on 16th May 1995 in Paris, France. Then later they took the marriage vows again in a civil ceremony at Richmond on 21st June. Before the marriage Jemima converted to Islam. On 18th November 1996, she gave birth to baby boy named Suliman Isa. Although Imran was born a Muslim he did not categorise himself to be a staunch follower of Islam. Imran Khan traces this lack of allegiance to Islam as a definite residue of the colonial hang over. In the post colonial Pakistan Imran said, "The Islamic class was not considered to be serious, and when I left school I was considered amongst the elite of the country because I could speak english and wore western clothes. Despite periodically shouting Pakistan Zindabad at school functions, I considered my own culture backward and Islam an out dated religion". Living between two cultures did not make things easier for Imran. At Oxford he began to see the exploitation of Islam by political activists. They practiced selective Islam in which the very essence of the religion was lost. This further drove Imran away from Islam. It was with the publishing of Salman Rushdie's Satanic Verses and the anti Islam allegations raged by the Muslim community that Imran was faced with a choice- either to fight or to flee. He decided to defend Islam as he realized that the attacks on Islam were unfair. Thus, started his odyssey to discover the spirit of Islam. To arm himself for the battle in defending Islam Imran read scholars like Ali Shariati, Mohammad Asad, Iqbal, Gai Eaton and the Holy Quran. This through reading of the Islamic texts gave a new direction to Imran's life. He said, ". . . I have become a better human being. . . . . . Almighty gave me so much to me, in turn I must use that blessing to help the less privileged. . "

Today Imran Khan lives in Lahore fully committed to realizing his dreams of a better Pakistan. He believes life is meant to be lived and that the past is over, the future does not exist and that the only time that really counts is the present. The essence of life is to move on. As the former captain put it, "I rarely want to sit back and talk about my cricketing days. That's over and finished with. . . I learnt a lot and then moved ahead."

Mother Teresa

It would not be inappropriate to call Mother Teresa "The Saint of the 20th century." Bent down in poised grace, with her white sari draping her head she was the very image of God's love on this earth. In turbulent times like ours where the race for materialism has all but completely wiped out our consciousness it was this apostle of love and mercy that was a beacon to millions all over the world. Her inspirational selfless work for the homeless, the poor, the aged, the handicapped and the unwanted was nothing short of the manifestation of the Divine Self.

Mother Teresa was born Agnes Gonxha Bojaxhiu on 26th August 1910 at Skopje in Macedonia. Her family belonged to the Albanian community. They were Catholics though the majority of the Albanians were muslims. Her father, Kole, was a well traveled businessman. Her mother, Drana, was a housewife. They had three children of which Agnes was the youngest. Unexpectedly when Agnes was nine her father died. Drana had to look after the family. She started to earn her living by sewing wedding dresses and doing embriodary. Inspite of these hardships theirs was a religious family. They prayed every evening, went to church everyday, prayed the rosary in may and assisted the service of the Holy Virgin. An annual pilgrimage to the place of Letnice, where Our Lady was venerated was a custom of the family.

This scriptural upbringing had a deep impact on Agnes. As a little girl she began to understand the quintessential meaning of the preachings of the gospel and this early in life she tried to put to practice what was preached. Her mother's influence in moulding the little Agnes into a deeply caring human being cannot be undermined. Apart from taking care of her three children, Drana much moved by the misery of an alcoholic woman in the neighbourhood started to take care of her. She went to wash and feed her twice a day. She began to take care of a widow and her six children. When Drana could not go, Agnes went to do this charitable work. On the death of the widow the children were raised in the Bojaxhiu household as a part of it. Thus, it was this exemplary attitude of her mother that instilled in Agnes the love and concern for others. This was to become so much a part of her character that leaving all other pleasures in later life. She was to completely devote herself to the well fare of the poor and the needy.

It was at the age of twelve that for the first time she felt a keen desire to spend her life doing God's work. But she was not sure. she prayed a lot and talked about it to her mother and sister. She even confided her earnest desire to a father at the Legion of Mary whom she had helped with learning a language.

"How can I be sure?," she said. He answered, ". . through your JOY. If you feel really happy by the idea that God might call you to serve Him, Him and your neighbour, then this is the evidence that you have a call. . . . the deep inner joy that you feel is your compass that indicates your direction in life".

Agnes was 18 when the decision was made. Over the last two years she had assisted several religious retreats in Lentice and it was clear to her that she would be a missionary in India. She then decided to join the Sisters of Our Lady of Loreto, who were very active in India. On 25th September 1928 she left for Dublin where the motherhouse of the Loreto Sisters is. Here Agnes learnt to speak english and was trained in religious life. On receiving the Sister's Habit she chose to call herself Sister Teresa in memory of the little Teresa of Lisieux, where they had stopped on the way to London. On 1st December 1928 Sister Teresa left for India to begin a new life.

After taking her vows at Darjeeling Sister Teresa dedicated herself to the care of the sick and the needy in a small hospital. Later she trained as a teacher and became the headmistress of a secondary school in the center of Calcutta. Not only did Sister Teresa teach the students History and Geography but she also took time to get to know the children personally and their families. She was loved by everyone who came in contact with her. So overwhelming was her concern for the children that they began calling her "Ma." Close to this institute were the slums of Calcutta. The miserable appalling conditions in which the poor lived wrenched her heart. Sister Teresa could turn away from such misery. Together with some girls she would visit the slums and try to help out the poor in any way that she could. But her contribution seemed insignificant to her in the face of such utter misery. During these years the Belgian Wallon Jesuit, Father Henry was a great source of inspiration to her.

To clear her tormented soul and to look for direction Sister Teresa went for a retreat to Darjeeling on the 10th of September 1937. Many years later Mother Teresa called it, "The most important journey of my life". It was here that she really heard God's voice. His message was clear: she had to leave the convent to help the poorest of the poor and to live with them. "It was an order, a duty, an absolute certainty. I knew what to do but I did not know how. "The 10th of September is called "Inspiration Day."

To leave the convent was not an easy matter. It had to be considered carefully. The matter was taken up by the Archbishop of Calcutta, mgr. Perier. The decision had to carefully analysed. The political situation at the time was precarious. India was about to gain independence. Questions like would a European be accepted after India became free? Would Rome approve of this decision? Sister Teresa was asked to wait for atleast a year before joining the Daughters of Saint Anna, sisters wearing a dark blue sari and working among the poor. Sister Teresa was disappointed. She did not simply want to work among the poor but wanted to live with the poor and the wait seemed endless. It was in August 1948 that she received the permission to leave the Loretto community by the Pope in Rome and the Mother General at Dublin.

Mother Teresa was 38 when she took the vows of poverty, purity and obedience. Giving up the Habit of the Sisters of Loretto, she took to wearing a cheap white sari with a blue border. Sister Teresa then went to Patna to train herself as a nurse. She realized the importance of such a training in her venture to help the poor who lived in dirt and unhealthy habitation. On completing her training Sister Teresa came back to Calcutta and began her life's vocation : to live among the poor and to help them. Soon she became a common figure in the slums and the streets of Calcutta. Her white sari, the fluent way in which she spoke Bengali and her unrelenting effort to improve the poor hygiene and literacy of the slums soon made her an endearing figure. Inspired by this lone European lady's dedication, one day a young Bengali girl who was a former student of Sister Teresa came to ask her permission to join her in this noble venture. The girl was from a well off family and Sister Teresa after explaining the hardships in this life of sacrifice asked the girl to consider her decision for a year and then to come back to her if she still wanted to be a part of the work. On 19th March 1949 the girl came back in all simplicity and earnest faith. She was the first to join Sister Teresa in her mission to improve the lot of the unwanted and the poor. Rising early at dawn the Sisters worked with faith and inner spiritual strength that comes with sincere prayer, as their only tool. At this time Sister Teresa so sure of the rightness of her vocation took Indian nationality. Her will to help the needy became stronger with each passing day.

With continuous work their community grew. Soon Sister Teresa began thinking seriously about starting a congregation. This was approved on 7th October 1950. Thus the "Constitutions of the Society of the Missionaries of Charity," came into being. It was the day of the feast of the Holy Rosary. After five years the congregation became papal as more and more Sisters joined the congregation and devoted their lives to the sick and the poorest of the poor.

At Calcutta owing to this growing numbers the Missionaries of Charity needed a residence. A Muslim leaving for Pakistan sold his house for a cheap price and this was to become the famous Mother's House at 54 A, Lower Circular Road, Calcutta. While the society grew the Mother's work kept increasing. Her work among the lepers of India, apart from being laudable in its own right got her international recognition. She received the Noble Prize for Peace in 1979. On receiving the honour Mother Teresa said, "I choose the poverty of our poor people. But I am grateful to receive (the Nobel) in the name of the hungry, the naked, the homeless, the crippled, the blind, the lepers, all those people who feel unwanted, unloved, uncared-for throughout society, people that have become a burden to society and are shunned by everyone."

On 5th September, 1997 Mother Teresa died of a heart attack at 9.30 in the evening. It was an irreplaceable loss felt world wide. Mother Teresa was buried on 13th September 1997, exactly 7 months after electing Sister Nirmala as her successor. The vacuum left by this Nirmal Hirday (Pure Heart) will never cease, Mother Teresa will live on in the memory of all those who were in her life time graced by her tender touch—that made all the difference.

Marilyn Monroe

Midst all the glamour and glittarati that the motion picture world provides the name of Marilyn Monroe stands supreme as the first most famous international sex symbol of the world. Oozing charm and charisma this nymph of the 50's had the whole world crooning at her feet. If money, beauty, fame be the measure of success then Marilyn Monroe had it all. Two generations later she still wears the crown of the sexiest woman of the 20th century. The choice is unanimous.

Born Norma Jean Mortenson on June 1, 1926, Marilyn's mother was a pretty red haired Hollywood cutter whose husband had left her. She then met Marilyn's father, a baker and Marilyn was born out of this casual union. Her father's itinerant behaviour and his subsequent abandoning of the mother when she broke the news of her pregnancy left painful scars of rejection that Marilyn could never come to terms with. As though illegitimacy was not a big enough cross to bear Marilyn's mother soon began to show signs of mental disturbance. She was committed to an institution. Thus, began the life of this rootless little orphan with all its share of insecurity, hurt, desolation and humiliation.

For the first few years Marilyn was transported to foster homes by the Country Welfare Agency. The foster parents were paid 20$ a month for the upkeep of this lost girl. At orphanages she earned a living by cleaning toilets. When she was seven or eight she was seduced by a border in her foster home. He gave her a nickel "not to tell. "On reporting the matter to her foster mother all she got was disbelief, suspicion and an admonishing for tarnishing the name of that "fine gentleman. "The seeds of insecurity were well sown. The security of a warm hearth was something Marilyn never knew. Guit ridden and worn by confused feelings of inadequacy Marilyn grew up with a low self esteem. These early insecurities became an integral part of her unconscious that though dormant were potent enough to shape her life. Marilyn recollecting her childhood said, "I always felt insecure . . . . But most of all I felt scared"

On approaching womanhood Marilyn discovered her one asset that would give her an edge over everyone else. It was her vital exuberant sexuality. "My arrival in school started everybody buzzing. . . . The boys began screaming and groaning." At last she had found a constant in her life that she could rely on. Her dazzling looks gave her confidence that she need not fear rejection any longer. For acceptance her beauty was her baton and she used it unsparingly. So hungry was she for acceptance and affection that she exploited her looks to an extent of what seemed a little short of promiscuity. When barely 16 she entered an ill matched marriage. Her husband and she separated after about two years apparently without success.

In 1944, while working on a defense plant Marilyn's natal stars began to shine. A United States Army photographer noticing her magnetic sex appeal induced her to pose for posters for the troops. An instant success as a model she was signed by a number of magazines as their 'Cover Girl.' She was signed by 20th Century-Fox for a small part. She worked briefly with Columbia Pictures in low budget musical films like Ladies of the Chorus (1949) and Love Happy (1949). At this time a failed love affair with a musical director raked her past insecurities and put her on the road to self annhilation. She attempted suicide. It was only the beginning of a spate of suicidal attempts the last of which was to take her life.

This golden tressed, curvaceous blond Love Goddess with a Maddona's face was the instant choice of Arthur Hornblow, Jr., and John Houston when they were looking for a face to fill a minor part in their film, The Asphalt Jungle. "As soon as we saw her we knew she was the one," recalls Hornblow. The virile voluptuousness of Venus combined with the quality of innocent depravity were what sent the audience pulsating to see more of her. She was recognized as that 'Calendar Girl' but instead of disowning her the public vied to never let her go. Her films like All About Eve (1950), Love Nest (1951), Clash By Night (1952) all hailed Marilyn Monroe as the Love icon of the century. In 1953 she received international fame for her roles in films like Niagra, How To Marry A Millionaire and Gentleman Prefer Blondes. 1954 saw her as the leading lady of Fox Productions.

Marilyn married the famous baseball player Joe Di Maggio in 1954. They divorced a year later. Rebelling against her long succession of stereotype roles she sought more challenging roles which a Fox contract offered her. In 1956 she married the playwright Arthur Miller. During the years of their marriage Marilyn said, "Now for the first time, I feel I am not alone anymore. I have a feeling of being sheltered. It's as if I have come in out of the cold. . . . ." Their marriage lasted four years.

Marilyn's years in stardom were beset with emotional highs and lows. Unending visits to psychiatrist and compulsive sucidal tendancies beset her life with depression. Beneath the veneer of bubbling callousness was a confused chaotic mind struggling to keep afloat. The fleeting years made her aware of her one enemy time. The ethereal beauty that so captivated the world had begun to wane and with that her only anchor of stability was fast diappearing. She was 36 and the mirror on the wall would not be able to hide the truth any longer. A lethal over dose of barbiturates in 1962 put an end to this saga of romance that had set the passions of millions on fire.

Marilyn's third husband Arthur Miller dramatized the tragedy of Marilyn Monroe in his play, After The Fall. Her acute sense of victimization was the direct residue of her precarious past. Her sense of vulnerability never allowed her to trust and to believe leading to failed relationships. She required "limitless" love and no man according to Miller is capable of it. A normal woman on maturing needs the reassurance of the mirror only marginally as the years go by. She relies more heavily on inner self confidence. This Marilyn lacked.

Perhaps deep down Marlilyn was still the little lonely Alice lost in the woods. So frightened was she of the gnomes and fairies of this world that lived through life without making any lasting contact with reality. She drifted in a make belief world of hers riddled with prejudice some justified and the rest of it unnecessary. This beautiful creature who was the envy of women and the fantasy of men all over died pathetically a lonely figure unaware that the world of love could have been hers if only she had not allowed the demons of distrust to take over and destroy her completely.

Helen Keller

The dawn of this century saw the working of determination and faith in the story of Helen Keller. Her's was the heart rending tale of a little girl who being afflicted with fever at 19 months lost not only her eyesight but her, hearing and speech as well. To conquer this triple handicap and to rise above such basic limitations was not only an arduous task but must have seemed an impossible one too. Today too with the hi-tech gadgetry that the modern day world can boast of it still seems quite a fantastic feat. But Helen Keller's diligence and fiercely invincible spirit has etched a story of success on the pages of history that inspires all humanity.

Born in the little Alabama town of Tuscumbia on 27 June, 1880, Helen was a beautiful healthy baby of her parents Captain Arthur Keller and his wife Katherine. Tragedy stuck, when Helen, a little over one and a half years lost her eyesight and hearing after she was stuck suddenly by a "fever of brain and stomach. "This rendered her to a life of total dependence . By the age of three Helen became mute as well. The happy gurgles of a child which are a mother's delight were never to be. Helen was sentenced to a life of silent dark loneliness the screams of which must go unheard.

Incarcerated in her prison of speechless sounds and blank darkness Helen's early childhood was characterized by temper tantrums. Unable to communicate her needs, desires, wishes and thoughts Helen was confined to a confused, frustated state of mind. Rebellion was the only successful way of effecting a response from the outside world. Shuttered in a tomb of silence and failing to make herself understood she gave in to wild gusts of rage that alienated her further from anyone who would otherwise have forwarded a hand of friendship. It seemed at that time that a life of seclusion bereft of a single ray of light or a single note of music was to be her lot. But hope came in the form of Annie Sullivan a graduate of the Perkins Institute for the Blind. Together, Helen and she were to make history.

Hope has a way of entering the penumbra of darkness and enlightening it. Helen's parents accepting their destiny, still waited for a miracle to happen. On reading Charles Dickens' American Notes, one day, Mrs Keller learnt about the much acclaimed Dr. Samuel Howe if the Perkins Institute for the Blind, in Boston. He had successfully instructed a deaf and dumb girl Laura Bridgman to read and write. Great expectations arose, only to be quelled as the troubled parents contacted the Perkins Institute for the Blind in desperation. Dr. Howe was dead. Thoroughly disappointed they saw the curtain falling on their hopes and plunging in darkness what started as a ray of light. It was then that the Greek born Dr. Michael Anagnos, Dr Howe's capable successor suggested the name of Anne Sullivan to try and teach the girl something.

Anne Sullivan's own life also had been far from happy. Born of Irish immigrant parents, her mother's death when Anne was eight and her father's abandonment of his three children there of, exposed Anne to a life of Harsh depravity. Anne was nearly blind from trachoma at the time and was sent to the Massachusetts State Infirmary. In 1880, she entered the Perkins Institute for the Blind and after two operations, she regained her eyesight to a workable level. But her eyes always were a source of trouble to her all her life. it was on graduating from the institute at the age of 21 that Anne was offered the assignment of Helen Keller.

Anne arrived at Alabama in 1886 with steadfast determination, seething under a patient demeanor. On arrival she encountered the trapped misery of her six year old ward. Unable to perform the everyday sundry actions like washing her face and buttoning her shoes, Helen's pathetic condition faced her with a formidable challenge. Anne's own experience with a handicap, equipped her well to understand the anguish of this tortured soul. To build a bond of trust was the first daunting task that Anne tackled. Anne handed a doll to the rampant child, made by the Perkins children. She made her first significant move by spelling the word d-o-l-l into Helen's hand. Helen was captivated by this novel move and soon she began to imitate Anne. The rapport between the student teacher was established. Anne noted of Helen, "Her restless spirit gropes in the dark. . . . . Her unsatisfied hands destroy whatever they touch-they do not know what else to do with things".

Helen's education began with her teacher getting to know the dark recesses of her troubled soul. Anne tried to understand the agony and ecstasy of Helen's life. She also began to understand Helen's attempt at communication. Anne started to teach Helen to spell words manually. Taking Helen to the pump house, one day Anne drew water. Pouring a mug of water on Helen's hand she spelled the word w-a-t-e-r into her hand. It was a startling revelation for Helen that everything had meaning. Excited with this new method of correlation, Helen pointed out to Anne in a questioning way. Anne then spelt the word t-e-a-c-h-e-r into her hand.

Thus at the age of six Helen Keller started to discover the vistas of the new world that opened before her. Years later Helen recollecting her 1st experience with the new world said, "Somehow the mystery of language was revealed to me. I knew that water meant the wonderful cool something that flowed over my hand. That living word awakened my soul, gave it light, hope, joy, set it free."

Helen learnt to read little sentences that Anne made possible by writing raised words next to their objects that Helen could identify. Within a few months Helen knew 625 words. Anne said, "The eagerness with which she absorbs ideas is delightful. "Helen also learnt to write beautifully and within a month of her training, she wrote a letter to her cousin in legible hand and correctly.

At the age of eight Helen was taken to Perknins institute by Anne. A new world of knowledge opened for Helen . Helen learnt of other people like her and nurtured new associations. She widened her social circle and formed new associations. She learnt Braille and voraciously poured over books from all walks of life. She communicated with other children who knew the manual alphabet. Both physically and mentally this was a very productive period for her. Helen traveled with Anne who painted an exact word picture for her of the gliding landscape, the booming cities, the different type of people and their different way of lifestyles. Helen's education widened and she understood the world around her in totality. Holidaying at Cape Cod, Helen discovered the world of sports. She learnt to swim, ride, row and sail.

In 1890, when Helen was 10 years old she learnt of a deaf, dumb and blind Norwegian girl who had been taught to talk. Anne took Helen there who met Sarah Fuller. the principal of the Horace Mann School for Deaf in Boston. Miss Fuller taking Helen's hand made her feel the movements of the jaw and teeth and tongue as she (Miss Fuller) spoke. She made sounds of "i" as in "it" several times. Helen picked up this technique and thus began her first tryst with speech. She learnt the vowels and soon she could distinctly speak the words mama and papa. Going home after her seventh lesson Helen said in "hollow, breathy tones"—"I am not dumb now."

Helen entered the Gilman School for Young Ladies at Cambridge and was heavily tutored. She entered Radcliff in 1900 and was the first individual with a triple handicap to enter the portals of this prestigious institution. Helen was 24 when she graduate with special honours in English. By this time she was a national celebrity. She was corresponding with well known figures like Graham Bell who not only was a keen admirer of her spirit but became a good friend to her. After training her voice she began giving public appearances to inspire people more fortunate than her. Her tall graceful personality full of charm and humour and her invincible spirit captivated the audience nation wide. Oliver Wendell Holmes wept when she Tennyson's "Break, break, break". In 1913, she made her first public appearence. "My mind froze," Helen recollected later. Though words rose to her lips, she was unable to utter even a single syllable at first. Then she uttered a single sound that sounded like a cannon ball going off, but it actually was only a whisper!

By 1914 Helen was an international speaker. She worked tirelessly for the blind, raising money for them and inspiring them through her own example. At this time a young Scottish girl, Polly Thompson joined them as their secretary and manager. Signing a contract with Hollywood they made the film Deliverence. Helen participated in vaudeville acts that she loved very much. She felt alive and refreshed at the close interaction that such a performance entailed. Helen wrote many books . Her books were published in many languages, as well as in Braille. She wrote, The Story of My Life (1902), The World I Live In (1908), Out of The Dark (1913), Midstream—My Later Life (1930), Let us have faith (1940), Teacher : Anne Sullivan Macy (1955), and The Open Door (1957). The motion picture The Unconquered (1954) and the play The Miracle Worker are based on her life. She visited many foreign lands and received rare honours in many countries. Helen's contribution to the handicapped after World War II, adds a generous dimension to her social work. She visited American hospitals and lectured in Europe on behalf of the physically handicapped.

In 1936 Anne died after a steady deterioration of her eyesight. It was a great loss to Helen who not only lost a teacher but a friend and a companion of a life time. Before her death someone said, "Teacher. . . . . get well. Without you Helen would be nothing."

"Then-then I have failed," Anne said. After Anne's death Helen picking up the reigns of life continued to make the world a better place for the blind all over the world. She became a pillar of strength for the American Foundation for the Blind. She lived with Miss Thompson in a picturesque hues set in the Connecticut woods near Westport with a stone Japanese lantern eight feet high constantly burning in a symbolic veneration of Helen's struggle. Helen died in 1968, just before her 88th birthday.

Abraham Lincoln

A bronzed, lank man! His suit of ancient black,
A famous high top-hat and plain worn shawl
Make him the quaint figure that men love,
The praire-lawyer, master of us all.

Vachel Lindsay
(Abraham Lincoln Walks At Midnight)

A century and a half later the name of Abraham Lincoln conjures up a legendary resonance to all those who hear it. It is a name spoken with reverence not only across the length and the breath of America but world wide. This celebrated national hero, heralded as Walt Whitman's "Captain" was indeed worthy of all the respect and regard that the land of prairies bestowed on him life based on handwork and conviction Lincoln's life was a journey from the log cabin to the White House. Taking up cudgels against Slavery, during his term as President of the United States, he ended this inhumane activity through the Thirteenth Amendment to the Constitution of the United States. Thus, giving the United States its unique blend of colossal breath and unity and an unchallenged position on the world map.

Abraham Lincoln descended from a family that were pioneers in moving west with the expanding country from Massachusetts through Pennsylvania to Virginia. They were wandering farmers who cleared the frontier of its wilderness and cultivated farms to give it character. After development the wander lust once again taking hold of them propelled them to other wilder pastures. Abraham Lincoln's father Thomas Lincoln followed the tradition of his ancestors and lived a full life as a frontier man moving from place to place. He developed as a skilled carpenter and never was in want of the necessities of life. Lincoln recollecting his father said that he, "even in childhood was a wandering boy labour boy, and grew up literally without education. He never did more in the way of writing than to bunglingly sign his own name." Abraham's mother Nancy was an illiterate woman from a poor Virginia family. She signed her name with an X.

On 12 Februray, 1809, in a log cabin on a farm south of Nolin Creek near what is now called Hodgenville, Kentucky Abraham Lincoln was born. He had an elder sister Sarah. Abraham Lincoln was only two when the family moved to another farm on nearby Knob Creek. Hunting, fishing, farming and household chores took up most of the time and there was hardly any time left to play. Life was hard. Due to confused administration and arbitrary justice Thomas Lincoln lost the title to his farmland. Disappointed in 1816, the Lincolns decided to move to Indiana where the land was surveyed and sold by the federal government. Sailing across the Ohio river they settled near Pigeon Creek, close to what is now Gentryville, Indiana. It was winter and Thomas Lincoln built a three sided shelter with a fire at the open end that kept them warm until he made a log cabin for the family. Heavily forested the place was not without apparent danger from the wild animals. Lincoln described it as a "wide region, with many bears and other wild animals in the woods." But soon the untamable wildness gave way to a thriving frontier community.

Abe had learnt the ways of the rugged frontier life. Clearing the forest for farmland was one of the most important tasks. Young Abe became adept at using the axe to fell trees. His strong frame and large built made it easy for him to handle what he later referred to as the "most useful instrument." He used it till he was twenty three years of age. He also used the axe to make fence rails by splitting poles. Years later as a presidential candidate Lincoln was known as the Railsplitter.

In 1818 tragedy struck the family. The raging epidemic at the time called 'milk-sick' struck Abraham's mother who died. The lack of immediate medical attention as the nearest doctor was 35 miles away and ignorance of the cause of the epidemic led to her immediate death. The disease it was discovered later was apparently caused by drinking milk from cows that had eaten the poisoned wild snake root plant.

The following year Thomas Lincoln journeying to Elizabethtown, married Sarah Bush Johnson, a widow with three children and a former sweetheart of Thomas Lincoln. She was a robust, brightfaced energetic woman with curly hair and a friendly face. The Lincoln children at once took to her. Abe became very attached to this stepmother and referred to her as "my angel mother." Her arrival brought order to the chaos of the Lincoln household. She understood the importance

71

of education and tried her best to educate these children in an environment that did not cater for mental development of its inhabitants. The physically demanding farm life made it difficult to spare Abraham for school life. But whenever time afforded Lincoln attended the ABC school. Such schools were held in log cabins where the teachers knew little more than the children themselves. According to Lincoln, "no qualification was ever required of a teacher beyond reading, writing, and ciphering, to the Rule of Three." Lincoln had less than one year of formal education in his entire life that too in fits and starts.

To the education given in the log cabin schools and to the unflagging encouragement given by his stepmother to learn Abraham learnt to read, write and do simple arithmetic quite early in life. His own interest in learning aided his quest for knowledge. He was able to read classical authors like Aesop, John Bunyan and Daniel Defoe as well as William Grimshaw's History of the United States (1820) and Mason Locke Weem's Life and Memorable Actions of George Washington (about 1800). The biography of the father of the nation left a lasting impression on Abraham who tried to emulate the ideals of this great man.

Young Lincoln grew to be a tall lad of about 6ft 4in. His long muscular body gave him an awkward appearance, though he had remarkable strength that came from hard labour. His father commenting on his appearance once said, "He looked as if he had been rough-hewn with an axe and needed smoothing with a jackplane." His early education and inherent intelligence gave him a way with words. His rustic humour and his ability to mimic made him a popular figure at the general store in nearby Gentryville. His easy congeniality was infectious. A neighbour affectionately recalled. "Abe was awful lazy, he would laugh and talk and crack jokes and tell stories all the time."

Lincoln's keen wandering mind looked for things to do that were beyond the humdrum of farming life. He found this opportunity when he was employed to ferry passengers and baggage to riverboats waiting midstream. At the age of 19 he was hired by a merchant James Gentry to take a cargo-laden flatboat down the Mississippi River to New Orleans. He thus experienced his first contact with the world outside the narrow defines of farming life.

Another 'milk sick' epidemic threatened to rage Indiana in 1830. The Lincoln family moved west to Illinois. Near what is now called Decatur, Illinois the Lincolns settled at a junction of woodland and prairie on the north bank of Sangamon. Lincoln together with his father built a log cabin for the family and fenced in 4 hectares of land to grow corn. He even hired himself to the other settlers to split rails.

It was here that Lincoln first attended a political rally. He was also coerced into speaking on behalf of the candidate. His first exposure to public speaking. A witness recalled that at first Lincoln was frightened but warmed up and eventually made the best speech of the day!

In 1831 Lincoln was hired by a Kentucky trader and speculator Denton Offutt. Lincoln along with his stepbrother and a cousin had to build a flatboat and take it down the Mississippi river with a load of cargo. Here was the first time Lincoln saw a slave auction that had a long lasting impact on his life. Seething with rage he said, "If I ever get a chance to hit this thing, I'll hit it hard." This early acquaintance with inhumane, terribly wrong practices parading as 'right' made Lincoln such a strong advocate for the abolishing of slave trade in America. His compassionate heart made him aware of the wretchedness of the system and made him a rightful candidate in emancipation of slaves.

Offutt much impressed with Lincoln's uprightness and his diligence hired him as a clerk in general store in New Salem. Lincoln earned 15$ a month plus the use of the store for sleeping. Lincoln's good humour, integrity and intelligence won him a place in the hearts of the people. His ability to take on the local ruffian in a local wrestling match carved a respectable position for him amongst the youth. His duties as a storekeeper provided ample time to read. Sprawled on the counter, book in hand and rolling off every now and then to serve a customer became a common sight. He improved his grammar by studying books on the subject. He discovered a new love for poetry and avidly read Robert Burns and William Shakespeare.

The store was also place for informal chit-chat. Lincoln would entertain his customers with the latest information from the newspaper who were in addition to hearing the news were only too delighted to hear him talk. Lincoln also joined the local debating society. A member had this reaction to Lincoln's first debate:"A perceptible smile at once lit up the face of the audience, for all anticipated the relation of some humourous story. But he opened up discussion in splendid style, to the infinite astonishment of his friends. . . . He pursued the question with reason and argument so pithy and forcibly that all were amazed."

James Rutledge the owner of a local tavern suggested a career in politics to the young Lincoln. Lincoln also came in contact with the attractive daughter of the tavern owner. Though much attracted to her charm and good nature he did not pursue his suit for she was said to be already engaged to a certain New Yorker called McNeil.

As a logical consequence, Lincoln decided to run for a seat in the Illinois house of representatives. In the meanwhile Lincoln found himself out of a job as the store he was working in went bankrupt. But the Black Hawk rebellion came just in time. Lincoln enlisted as a volunteer to quell the rebellion of the Native American Sauk and Fox led by their chief Black Hawk. His popularity made him head the company he was enlisted in. When his term expired, he reenlisted as a private. Though he saw no actual fighting, Lincoln was very proud of his career in the army.

In 1832 he contested for the Illinois seat. He was defeated. He then opened a general store with an acquaintance William Berry. But Berry misused the profits and in a few months they were running in a loss. Berry died in 1835, leaving Lincoln responsible for debts amounting to 1100$. It took Lincoln several months/years before he cleared these debts. He then began a short stint as the Postmaster at New Salem which earned him $60 a year plus a percentage of receipts on postage. He even became the deputy surveyor of Sangamon County.

Lincoln contested the legislative elections in 1834 and was elected. He was reelected in 1836, 1838 and 1840. At this time he heard that Ann Rutledge had been jilted in love. She was sick and before dying had asked to see Lincoln. Legend has that Ann was the one love of his life and that he never actually got over this loss. His later bouts of melancholy have been attributed to this loss. In the meanwhile Lincoln continued to study law and in 1836 he was admitted to the bar as a licensed attorney. He moved to Springfield.

By certain unknown circumstances Lincoln became engaged to a Kentucky girl called Mary Owens. But the engagement broke, much to Lincoln's relief it is believed. Later Miss Owens is said to have said, "I thought Mr. Lincoln was deficient in those little links that make up the chain of a woman's happiness." On 4th November1842 he married another Kentucky girl, Mary Todd. She was high strung and a member of the local aristocracy. A week after the wedding he wrote, "Nothing new here, except my marrying, which to me is a matter of profound wonder." His wife's whimsical, vain ways were a definite contrast to the sweet natured Ann Rutledge. Their marriage always beset by arguments could never be termed as "well matched", except for their sharing of ambition. Mary played a key role in aiding and supporting her husband's political career. The Lincoln's had four boys out of which only Richard Todd Lincoln reached adulthood.

Though still a practicing lawyer, Lincoln stove to achieve his political ambitions. He began to look beyond the statehouse to the seat in the US Congress. In 1843, he wrote to a fellow politician, "Now if you should hear anyone say that Lincoln don't want to go to Congress, I wish you as a personal friend of mine, would tell him you have reason to believe he is mistaken. The truth is I would like to go very much." Lincoln sought the nomination for the US representative, for the Seventh Congressional District in 1842 and. 1844. He received it in 1846. He defeated the Democratic candidate, the Methodist preacher Peter Cartwright, in the election of November 1846. In 1847 he went to Washington.

The question of slavery always haunted Lincoln. He became a forceful spokesman for anti slavery and in faith introduced the bill for the abolition of slavery in the District of Columbia, during the second session. The bill was rejected and Lincoln returned to Illinois disappointed. He was not reelected the following term.

The bombardment of Fort Sumter, by the Carolinians was a testing time for Lincoln. Using the language and authority of militia act of 1795, he declared that in seven states the federal laws were opposed. He asked the remaining loyal states for 75,000 militia for three months tenure. The Civil War had begun. By virtue of a constitutional clause he was the Commander in Chief of the US Army and Navy. He said, "I suppose I have a right to take any measure which may subdue the enemy." His most competent general during the war was Ulusses. S. Grant who drank whiskey and fought like a lion. In characteristic dry humour Lincoln asked, "Do you know what brand of whiskey I'd like to send a barrel to each of my other generals."

In 1854, denouncing the Kansas-Nebraska Act, Lincoln attacked Stephen. A. Douglas, a democrat and the supporter of the act. For Lincoln slavery was both a moral and a political issue. Highlighting the sheer injustice of the Act, he said, "It is said that the slaveholder has the same political right to take his Negroes to Kansas, that a freeman has to take his hogs or his horses. This would be true if Negroes were property in the same sense that hogs and horses are. But is this the case? It is notoriously not so." In autumn that year Lincoln was elected to the legislature but lost the United States Senate seat.

Secession from the Union of the Southern slave owning states was becoming a burning issue. In 1858, the Republican Party gaining momentum declared Lincoln as "our first and only choice" for US Senator. Lincoln was defeated. But by May 1860, Lincoln's speeches in New York had gained him a national reputation. He was nominated as a candidate for presidency. He was elected and on 4th March 1861, Lincoln took over the office of the President of the United States. In the winter of 1861 the Union became involved with Great Britain in the trent Affair. The Confederacy sent James Murray Mason and John Slidell to Britain and France to support the Southern cause. When aboard the British ship Trent, the ship was stopped and searched by a Union naval captain, Charles Wilkes and the two southerners were taken prisoners. Britain demanded an apology and midst much ado Lincoln complied and apologised. He thus averted war with Britain. The Civil War continued to rage through Lincoln's first term at office. He was nominated for the second term and was reelected. Supporting his stance on the Civil War he said, "This is essentially a people's contest.

. . to demonstrate to the world that those who can fairly carry out an election can also suppress a rebellion; and ballots are the rightful successors to bullets. . . . . . "

At first Lincoln had believed in gradual emancipation. But gradually he came to believe in complete emancipation. His views on anti slavery were clear. To him slavery was incompatible with American democracy. He said, "When the white man governs himself, that is self-government;but when he governs another man, why then my ancient faith teaches me that 'all men are created equal, ' and that there can be no moral right in connection with the man's making a slave of another."

General Lee of the Confederate surrendered and the war came to an end with the Union flag raised high over Fort Sumter on 14th April to the thundering guns. Lincoln though an adversary respected Lee's total commitment to a cause and his enviable soldiering. Paying tribute to the photograph of this hero of the Southern states he said, "It is a good face, the face of a noble brave man. I am glad the war is over at last."

The aftermath of war saw Mrs. Lincoln plunging into much awaited hectic social activity. She cruised through the social scene making up for lost time. The war had offered little opportunity to parade as the first lady. An evening at the Ford Theater was arranged to see Laura Keen in a play, "Our American Cousin". The Lincoln's arrived and took their place in the flag draped box. Tired and exhausted after the grueling hours of wartime America, the piece of entertainment must have been a good change for the Lincoln's -to begin with. The nightmare began when softly into the box came a dark shadow. Shooting the President at point blank range the man disappeared into the folds of darkness. Midst smoke and uproar the wounded President was rushed to a house across the street and immediate medical attention followed. At 7 o'clock in the morning the next day he was declared dead.

John Wilkens Booth, Lincoln's assassin and a supporter of the southern cause was shot down in a barn a few days later.

The country was shrouded in intangible darkness as the endless number of mourners join the funeral procession from Washington to Springfield. Walt Whitman's "star" had fallen and the lilacs had for the last time bloom'd in the dooryard.

Bill Gates

Bill Gates, the software magnet holds not only an enviable position in the business world today but is the acclaimed genius of our times. As the American business executive officer of the Microsoft Corporation, Gates dominates the world of hi tech computers.

Born at Seattle, Washinton in 1955, Gates father was a lawyer and his mother a strong willed, outgoing lady. Gates in contrast was a shy boy. He preferred the company of his own thoughts. Unlike his mates Gates was far more concerned with the magic of numbers than fast cars and movie mania. He would spend hours alone and in tie his parents became concerned about the little boy. His father recalling Bill's childhood says, "He was so small and shy, in need of protection and his interests were so different from the children of his age." Gates at the time was in the sixth standard. Often, when asked, "What are you doing?" the standard reply would be, "I'm thinking."

Bill's rationale and a fiercely competitive spirit where "winning mattered" was nurtured in early childhood. Large family dinners were often followed by organized bridge games and trivia. These, Gates recalls were played seriously. He was nicknamed 'Trey' (three in card terminology).

Even as a boy Gates' interests were different from others. Instead of following the normal run of the mill activities, Trey often spent time thinking about the numbers and their varied behavioral pattern. At a small school where he studied he first came in contact with the world of computers. It was a teletype computer terminal.

By his 13th year Gates and his close friend Paul Allen had picked up computer language from a manual. In the eighth standard Bill had to his credit two programmes. One of then dealt with conversion of one mathematical base into another base. The second programme was a game of noughts and crosses. Later he devised a computer version of RISK, a board game with the final aim of world domination.

Trey's novel interest gave him an exposure into the world of men where work was done with a serious intent. With his friend Paul, Trey spent hours at local company with a new computer. They had to identify the "bugs", that would crash it. Often Trey would sneak out after his parents went to bed and spent most of the night at the company. He did maximum overtime and his reward was pleasure!

While work was pleasure, persuing of leisure was an arduous task for the reticent Bill. Gates lacked confidence in social settings all through his early years. It was only in high school that the shackles of self consciousness began to give away. Getting places in the top 10 of the US aptitude exam and his meritous mental ability amongst his comrades gave him the required confidence. At this point "his confidence and sense of humour increased, "his father recalls. He even worked out programmes that would put him in classes with the 'right' girls.

It was at Harvard that Bill Gates met Steve Ballmer. Both took postgraduate level courses and Ballmer nurtured Gates' social side. Under Ballmer's influence Gates joined the college eating club and started to visit popular discos in New York. In 1980 Ballmer joined Microsoft. Gates says, "I always would have close business associates like Ballmer and several of the other top people at Microsoft, and that we would stick together and grow together no matter what happened."

While attending Harvard in 1975, Gates teamed with Allen to develop a version of the BASIC computer programming language for the ALTAIR, the first personal computer. This led to the formation of Microsoft in Albuquerque, New Mexico, in the same year. Gates decided to drop out of Harvard in 1977 to work at Microsoft full-time, persuing his vision of "a computer on every desk and in every home." In 1979 Gates and Allen moved the company to Redmond, Washington, a suburb of their hometown of Seattle. Since then the Microsoft has grown from 15 employees and $500,55 in revenues in 1978 to over 20,000 employees and $5.9 billion in revenues for the fiscal year in June 1995.

In 1981 Microsoft took its first step in diversifying beyond the programming languages market when it released MS-DOS, the operating system for the original IBM personal computer (PC). Microsoft went on to convince other PC manufacturers to license MS-DOS, which made it the de-facto software standard for PCs. Microsoft collaboration with IBM throughout 1980s created the world's first mass-market phenomenon in the computer industry based on the availability of computer chips, parts and the MS-DOS operating systems. The acceptance of the MS-DOS as the software standard for the PC led to Microsoft's increasingly important role in the industry.

Microsoft is a sprawling campus of 35 low rise buildings where competitive workers work relentlessly to materialize Gates' dream, perhaps of world domination. To Microsoft goes the credit of growing the market in desk top operating systems. They survived companies like IBM, which are 10 times their size.

Dressed in khaki trousers and flannel shirts the young members of the Microsoft world are called "Bill clones. "These are brilliant young minds hired to be trained in the combined art of technical brilliance and creativity. At the entrance test they are subjected to a rigorous IQ test that poses all but easy questions.

One of the routine tasks of Gates at the Microsoft is to hold meetings with teams working on various projects. The teams are subjected to grilling questions on politics of their rivals, details of technology, marketing strategy and so on. No area remains untouched. Gates expects only excellence from his teams. There is no place for second rate outputs. A good set of ideas is unhesitatingly termed as "really neat"or "supercool. "The bad strategies are unsparingly labeled as "crummy", "really dumb" or "random to the max".

Gates office like the man himself is shrouded in silence most of the time. The phone almost never rings. Most of his contact to the outside world is through e-mail. The office is sparsely decorated with ordinary furniture with a lot of airy room for thought.

Gates hopes to run Microsoft for another decade or so. After that he plans to give 95% of his wealth away. Warren Buffett, the investor whom Gates demoted to the second richest says that Gates, ". . . will spend time thinking about the impact his philanthropy can have. . . . . He is too imaginative to do conventional gifts."

Gates married Metilda French in 1994. She was working for the company when he met her at one of the Microsoft press conferences. She is intelligent and independent and spends most of her time devoted to charity work now. The Gates have already given away $34 million to the University of Washington; $15 million for a new computer center at Harvard University; $6 million to Stanford University; $3 million in book royalties to the National Foundation for Improvement of Education to fund innovative technology programmes in US schools and $200 million to a foundation run by his father.

Jennifer, a daughter was born to the couple in April 1996. Gates, friends say is smitten by this new love of his. Talking about his fatherhood he says, "I used to think I wouldn't be at all interested in the baby until she could talk. . . . . But I am totally into it now. She's just started to say 'ba-ba' and have a personality". He jokingly adds that there is something other than Netscape keeping him awake at night!

Although Jennifer's birth may have tempered the fiercely competitive spirit he still pushes hard and is known to be a Darwinian at heart. A former Microsoft executive and an admirer cum a critic points out, "He doesn't look for win-win situations, but for ways to make others lose. Success is defined as flattening the competition, not creating excellence. In Bill's eyes he's still the kid whose afraid he'll go out of business if he lets anyone compete." Countering the view that what drives Bill is a sense of paranoia Nathan Myhrvold, 37 says, "Bill is not threatened by intelligent people. . . . . . only stupid ones." For

Gates competition is a sport and one must play it with verve and alacrity. He calls it "superfun."

The 43 year old big boss of the bit and byte with a passion for speeding and intelligent minds is much matured man. Less enamoured with pure intelligence than before he says, "I don't think that IQ is as fungible as I used to. To succeed you have to know how to make choices and how to think more morally."

This giant of the computer world has a lot of years ahead of him. With his marked ability to translate technical vision into market strategy and to blend creativity with technical acumen, we can look forward to a future of stupendous innovation, that not only sharpens our grey cells but will have us crying for more.

Albert Einstein

The name Einstein has become synonymous with the word 'genius'. The greatest scientist of this century, Albert Einstein's theories brought about a revolution in the world of thinking men. His theories were profound, although his ideas stemmed from common everyday occurances. A walk on the wet sands of a beach reminded him of surface tension, the elastic-skin effect of a liquid surface, that holds a drop together. This ability of going to the heart of the matter is what made Einstein rock the world of physics and mathematics with the theory of relativity and the quantum theory of light. The seemingly contradictory theories where one claimed that light consists of waves and the other said that it somehow consists of particles were proposed all at once. It was a revolutionary breakthrough in the world of science. Much of science is indebted to this unassuming German Jew with a soft manner and a brilliant mind.

Born on 14th March 1879 in the town of Ulm in Wurttemberg, Einstein was no child progidy. Infact he did not learn to speak until the age of three and his parents feared that he might be a dullard. At school he was considered average until he taught himself calculus and the teachers began to fear facing his staggering questions.

When Einstein was barely one year old his parents moved to a large south German town of Munich. There in partnership with his brother, Einstein's father opened a small electro-chemical factory. Here Einstein spent his early childhood. Under the tutelage and influence of his Uncle Einstein developed a keen interest in maths and physics. Together they explored the mysteries of the algebraic and mathematical numbers. Young Einstein inherited the love for music from his mother. He was an accomplished amateur musician and played the violin. He preferred the music of Mozart to Beethoven for he felt that while Beethoven "created" music, Mozart "found" music.

Einstein's family migrated to Milan when he was 15 years old. He was left behind to complete his studies at the Luitbold Gymnasium. But the regimentation of the school's curriculum did not appeal to his bohemian soul and with the sunny shores of Italy beckoning him he left for Milan. He joined his parents only to find that his father had gone bankrupt. He then migrated to Switzerland. He failed his entrance examination at the reputed Swiss Federal Polytechnic School in Zurich, the first time. The next year he was admitted. Here, he met a young Hungarian girl, Mileva Maritsch. They shared a passion for physics and often spent hours working on the problems posed by physics. On leaving the Polytechnic they got married. But unfortunately Einstein discovered that beyond the world of physics they had little in common. It was the birth of two sons that kept them together for many years.

On leaving the Polytechnic Einstein acquires Swiss citenship. By this time he was very much in love with the pristine Swiss mountains. He found a job in the patent office at Berne. His job entailed him to investigate every invention. He then had to pick out basic ideas from these and put them accurately on paper. It left him plenty of time to pursue his studies. The first recognition came his ways when Einstein published his papers on the production and transformation of light on the electro-dynamics of moving bodies in 1905. His talent was recognized and he was at once given the post of junior professor at the University of Zurich.

At the University, Einstein simple man had to live up to social standard of department that his intellectual mind found hard to cope with. The family had a hard time, "keeping appearances". This was difficult with the limited salary that he earned. Years later recounting his days at Zurich Einstein jokingly remarked, "In my Relativity I set up a clock at every point in space - but in reality, I found it difficult to provide even one in my room. "One of the most remarkable traits of Einstein was his down to earth attitude. Though having seen financial hardship, he continued to be content with the bare minimum. Greed or a desire for materialism was foreign to him.

On being invited to the Institute for Advanced Study at Princeton many years later when he was a renowned personality, he was offered carte blanche as salary. Einstein asked for an impossible sum; it was far too small. The director of the institute had to plead with him to accept atleast a decent salary. Such was the simplicity that this great man exuded.

In 1911, he went to Prague on a better paid post as a proffessor. Being part of the Jewish ethos for the first time

Einstein was exposed to anti-Semetism. He subsequently went back to Zurich and taught at the Polytechnic for two years.

By this time Einstein was a scientist of international repute. He gained membership of the Royal Prussian Academy of Science and the directorship of the Kaiser Wilhelm Institute at Berlin. Here he met his happy -go-lucky distant cousin Elsa Einstein and fell in love with her. He married her. They enjoyed a fulfilling relation until her death in 1936. Einstein grieved, but it was his pre-occupation with his work that made him cope with the sudden vacuum in his life. At the time of his wife's death a polish physicist Leopald Infeld and Banesh Hoffman were working with Einstein. Hoffman, visiting Einstein at the time recalls a haggard, grief lined man. Subtly, by way of consolation, Hoffman veered the conversation to an absorbing discussion about physics. He intended to distract Einstein however momentarily from his present grief. Einstein soon was absorbed in the discussion and time flew that day. Hoffman's kindness did not escape Einstein. As Hoffman was about to leave, Einstein in a voice filled with emotion said, "It was a fun. "This was Einstein's way of saying thank you."

Einstein though a radical bohemian in the sense of not adhering to any faith, was the ". . . most religious man I have known," said Hoffman. Einstein believed that ideas came from God and that the law of the Universe laid down by God was subtle but not malicious. The puzzling contradictions that the universe presented were natural. They were there to goad man to "tink" (think). A heavy accent prevented the formation of the sound "th". When facing a quaint problem Einstein would pace up and down, twirling a lock of long greying hair around his forefingers and smoked a pipe. Minutes would pass in silent communion with the inner working of his mind for a few minutes before he came up with an answer.

After 1919, Einstein became an internationally renowned figure. He was conferred with honours and awards wherever he went. He received the Noble Prize in 1921 but the selection committee had to avoid mentioning relativity which was highly controversial at the time and pretended to give him the prize for his work on the quantum theory. With the Nazi reign of terror his theories were declared false, for they came from a Jew. Apart from confiscating his property it has been rumoured that a price was put on his head.

Zionism and Pacifism claimed a good deal of Einstein's attention. During World War I, he was one of the few academics to publicly decry Germany's involvement in the war. After the war his continued public support of the pacifist and Zionist goals made him the target of viscious attacks by anti-Semetic and right wing elements in Germany.

When Hitler came to power Einstein decided to leave Germany. He migrated to the US. There, he joined the Institute for Advanced Study at Prinston, New Jersey. Here, he continued to support Zionism but renounced his pacifist stand in the face of the awesome threat to humankind posed by the Nazi reign of terror. In 1939 Einstein collaborated with several other physicists in writing a letter to President Franklin D Roosevelt. The letter alerted the US Govt. to Germany's potential and likelihood in making an atomic bomb. This in turn ironically plunged the Roosevelt administration into making their own atomic bomb. Einstein unaware of this was utterly dismayed to hear of the agony and destruction that his $E=mc^2$ had wrought.

After the war, Einstein was active in the cause of international disarmament and world govt. He continued to support Zionism but declined the offer made by the leaders of the state of Israel to become president of that country. In the US during the late 1940s and early 50s he spoke out on the need for the nation's intellectuals to make any sacrifice necessary to preserve political freedom. Einstein died in Princeton on April 18, 1955.

His writings include Relativity : The Special and General Theory (1916); About Zionism (1931); Builder of the Universe (1932); Why War? (1933) with Sigmund Freud; The World As I See (1934), with the Polish physicist Leopald Infeld; and Out of My Later Years (1950).

Today, on the threshold of the 21st century, when it comes to paying a tribute to this great man who delved deep into concepts of time and space. His findings on time gave a new dimension to the concept. It was explosive and controversial. This is what made Einstein so important. As one Noble Prize Winner trying to convey the magical quality of Einstein's achievement stood before a waiting audience and found that the words eluded him. They were celebrating Einstein's 70th birthday at Princeton. Embarrassed at his ineloquence, in desperation he pointed out at his watch and said, "It all came from this." As Hoffman later put it, "His very ineloquence made this the most eloquent tribute I ever heard to Einstein's genius."

Charlie Chaplin

If one happens to see a man wearing baggy trousers, enormous shoes, a bowler hat, carrying a bamboo cane and strutting around in acrobatic elegance, then one can be rest assured that the man on the celluloid screen is none other than '*The Tramp*' of the 1920s, portrayed by Charles Spencer Chaplin or Charlie Chaplin as he is popularly known. The portrayal of '*The Tramp*' was a universally recognized symbol of indestructible individuality, triumphing over adversity and persecution, both human and mechanical. This won him great acclaim as the tragi-comedian of the silent movie era.

Before the sonorous entering of sound into the cinematic world Charlie Chaplin's individual style of performing, derived from the circus clown and mime, combined with expressive gesture, facial eloquence and impeccable timing had the world swooning for more of Chaplin's dramatic art. His stupendous performance changed gave a face lift to the slapstick and changed the jaunty stereotype into a compassionate human figure loved world wide. Chaplin's treatment of his subjects compounded satire and pathos. It revealed a love of humanity and individual freedom.

Ironically this king of comedy who had the audience rolling on their seats had a woeful past. He was born on 16 April, 1889 at London to poor parents. They were music hall artists. After struggling to make ends meet, Chaplin's father an alcoholic, would spend the money on drink, to the dismay of his family. This put responsibility on Chaplin and he was pushed on stage when he was barely five. His father's untimely death and his mother's lack of good health made orphans cf the little children. Charlie and his brother Sid found themselves in an orphanage until their mother recovered sufficiently to look after them. She worked hard and began to support her family by sewing blouses.

To supplement the family's income Charlie joined a touring music hall act, "*The eight Lancashire Lads*", at the age of seven. After working for a year he joined school for two years. This was the only formal education he ever had in his life. Soon his mother's mental health once again began to deteriorate and he found himself once again at the mercy of providence. By this time his brother had left for the sea and Charlie for a few months led a life of a waif midst the dirt and squalor of London streets. The experience left an indelible mark on the young impressionistic mind of the young Charlie. Years later in a poignant portrayal of a young waif (played by Jackie Coogan) Chaplin recreated his long buried past.

In 1910, Chaplin toured the United States with a pantomime troupe and decided to remain in the country. At first he acted in small parts in plays like Peter Pan, Jim, Sherlock Holmes, the Romance of a Cockney and other famous theater plays of the time.

By 1913, Chaplin was already a rated comedian of the famous Fred Karno Company. But the upheaval in the cinema world where American companies fearing foreign competition plunged into making "feature-length" films instead of the short two reelers. The market was open with a demand for fresh actors. Screen adaptations were the pulse of the day. Chaplin ceased this opportunity and bid farewell to Karno's company. Even theaters like Broadway saw a general exodus of actors in search of greener pastures.

Chaplin got a break at the Keystone company at hundred and fifty dollars a week. This was three times the salary he got as a theatre artist. At Keystone Mack Sennett was the producer. His basic focus was on slapstick. The enormously popular Keystone Kops who were a bunch of incompetents and who never could nab their man is welknown. Charlie's entrance into the studio which was a vast open platform covered with muslin sheets for diffused lighting was to begin with not encouraging. Slapstick was not really Chaplin's style. His training as a pantomime artist had made him a more subtle performer for whom a twitch of the eyebrow and and a flick of a muscle was as important as a man falling on a banana peel! He found acceptance amongst his company workers also slow to come. But it was his friendship with the two comedians Arbuckle and Swain that kept him afloat during these hard times.

"Making a Living" was his first film at Keystone. He wore a frock-coat, top hat, walrus moustache and eyeglasses. It took one week to produce the film and Chaplin received moderate success.

It was with the film "*Kid Auto Races at Venice*", that Chaplin was showered with accolades that his talent most deserved. In this film he wore the famous 'Charlie Chaplin' costume that won the hearts of millions around the world.

Providence and chance played key roles, in placing Chaplin on the world stage. Sennett, the Keystone producer was in a habit of putting spare actors and actress in the foreground of public gatherings. He would at times even shoot a short film with the crowd in the background. It would save him the expense of the "extras." It was for such a public occasion of a children's auto race at a sea side resort of Venice, outside Los Angeles that Charlie found himself detailed. He was to improvise a comic film of about quarter of an hour's duration. For assembling such a comic costume, he borrowed from Fatty Arbuckle and Ford Sterling the famous costume that would take him to world fame. Thus, was born the idolatry figure, "The Tramp" that would enthrall the world with its performance for many years to come. This 45 minutes film of dashing on the racetrack, getting in the way of the dummy camera and being persuaded by the Keystone Kops, established Chaplin's reputation internationally. Chaplin wore the same costume for the next 25 years in 70 films.

Within one year Chaplin signed a contract with Essanay Films for twelve hundred and fifty dollars a week. Later Mutual signed him for ten thousand dollars a week.

While working in Shoulder Arms, a satire on army life, Chaplin met Mildred Harris, a sixteen year old actress. Chaplin fell hopelessly in love with her and married her that October. The following year a son was born to them. He died three days later. Chaplin never could get over the loss of his "Little Mouse." His marriage from then on was a disaster. Chaplin later married another young actress called, Lita Grey. A son Charles Spencer Chaplin Jr. was born to them, followed by a second son Sydney

Earl Chaplin. The marriage like the previous one failed and Charles was quoted by Lita herself, as saying, "Well boys this is better than the penitentiary, but it won't last." Perhaps, Chaplin's near fatal attraction for the young girls and their difficulty in understanding the older more complex man they were married to was the raison d'etre for the failure in matrimony. In 1927 they divorced and Lita received 600$ by way of compensation. He then married and divorced the actress Paulette Goddard. In 1943, at the age of 54 Chaplin married the 18 year old daughter of the well known playwright Eugene O'Neil. At last he found matrimonial bliss.

In 1919 Chaplin helped found the United Artists Corporation, with which he was associated with until 1952. Important pictures Chaplin produced and starred in include *The Kid* (1921), *The Pilgrim* (1923), *The Gold Rush* (1925), *The Circus* (1928), *City Lights* (1931), *Modern Times* (1936), *The Great Dictator* (1940), *Monsieur Verdoux* (1947), *Limelight* (1952), and *A Key in New York* (1967). He composed background music for most of his films. The Gold Rush was probably the most celebrated film of Charlie Chaplin's carrer. According to Chaplin it was, ". . . the picture I want to be remembered by."

In 1921, the year The Kid was released Chaplin taking a trip down the memory lane visited London. He received an overwhelming reception in the same streets that had once shunned him when as waif he was out alone in the cold, many years back. He was knighted in 1975.

The *City Lights* was perhaps Chaplin's greatest films. It confirmed Chaplin's position as a creative intellectual genius of the world cinema. Despite Chaplin's lack of formal education he was very receptive to ideas. When D.W. Griffith's Birth of a. Nation came to Los Angeles he made it a point to see it many times to understand the subtleties thoroughly.

Chaplin was criticized for his leftist political views. He migrated to Switzerland in 1952. In 1972 he briefly returned to the United States and received several tributes, among them a special Academy Award for special contribution to the film industry. He died in 1977.

Chaplin's legend lives on as hundred's of movie loving people all around the world throng to see the funny "little man" and buy a laugh for a few dollars. Crediting him as an "entertainer supreme" would only be an understatement.

John F Kennedy

   John F Kennedy, the 35th president of the United States
was also the youngest president elect of the country. His
charismatic charm is legendary and as in his lifetime even
today he's counted amongst the most popular icons of the
past, and is subject to the same idolatory. His intellectual
excellence together with sagacious handling of the Cuban
Missile crises, amongst other things, got him international
recognition. No other President since has enjoyed such a
concentrated fanfare, as this young President whose words at
the inaugural address had have gone in the pages of history
for posterity to quote and requote, "Ask not what your country
can do for you-ask what you can do for your country." He held
the torch of a new generation of Americans who, were born in

this century, who were tempered by war and disciplined by hardwork and bitter peace.

Born on 29 May, 1917, in Brooklyn Massachusetts, John was the second of the nine children of Joseph Patrick Kennedy and his wife, Rose Fitzgerald Kennedy. They were a wealthy business family with a background in politics. Rose Kennedy was the daughter of John F. Fitzgerald, who as a mayor of Boston Massachusetts, was popularly known as "Honey Fitz." Joseph Kennedy was the son of Patrick Kennedy a successful businessman as a prominent Boston politician. It was the Kennedy's plan to send their first born Joseph Kennedy Jr., into politics. But, fate had different plans and Joseph K. Jr. was killed in World War II. The next in line was John who fulfilled his father's dream of not only joining politics but also becoming the first Roman Catholic president of the United States. Later, as a US Senator, Kennedy said, "Just as I went into politics because Joe died, if anything happens to me tomorrow, my brother Bobby would run for my seat in the Senate. And if Bobby died, Teddy would take over from him." How true these words would ring within a few years of their being uttered was perhaps unfathomable to even John Kennedy who, though speaking with conviction, never imagined that it would all be only too tragically true.

Kennedy at the age of 13 went to the Canterbury School, a private school in New Milford, Connecticut for a short while. An illness cut short his term there. He later graduated from Choate Preparatory school in Wallingford, Connecticut and in 1935 he entered Princeton University. Once again the onset of an illness forced him to leave school and the following year he joined Harvard University. Despite ill health, John Kennedy was a good athelete. He proved himself to be an ace swimmer and an outstanding sailor.

Kennedy was intellectually oriented. His undergraduate thesis at Harvard culminated in a book, Why England Slept (1940). It was in-depth study of Great Britain's response to German rearmament prior to World War II. The book gained attention in England and U.S. Kennedy graduated in 1940. He then attended Stanford University's business school for a while and then traveled to South America.

In 1939 World War II broke out and the US entered the war with Japan's attack on Pearl Harbour. Kennedy, like all young Americans aspired to join the U. S army but was rejected on account of a spine injury incurred during a football game at Harvard. But, after irreligiously pursued keep fit programme Kennedy was selected in the US Navy.

Early in 1943 Kennedy became commander of PT Boat 109 in the South Pacific. In August 1943 the boat was rammed by a Japanese destroyer in the waters off New Georgia in the Solomon Islands. The boat was sliced in half and two of the twelve men aboard were killed. Kennedy and the other survivors clung for hours to the werckage, hoping for rescue. When none came they swam to a small island 5km away. Kennedy towed a wounded crew member by clutching the long strap of the injured man's life jacket between his teeth. For the next four days Kennedy swam along a water route he knew American ships used. He finally encountered friendly natives on Cross Island. They brought his message for help carved on a coconut shell, to the U.S. Infantry Patrol and Kennedy and his crew were finally rescued. Kennedy received the US Navy and Mariene Corps medal for, "courage, endurance and excellent leadership." Ill health once again made him leave the army and return to the US.

At the age of 29, Kennedy won the Democratic nomination in the 11th Congressional District of massachusetts. He served three terms in the House of Representatives, all during the

Democratic administrations of President Harry. S Truman. His recent heroic record and his concentrated meetings of the voters won him the elections. During his term as a senator he backed legislation beneficial to the Massachusetts textile, fishing, watch and transportation industries.

In 1953, Kennedy married Jacqueline Lee Bouvier. Less than a year after his marriage Kennedy underwent a spiral-disk operation. Four months after a painful convalescence, a second term operation was performed. It was at this time that Kennedy wrote Profiles in Courage that won him the Pulitzer Prize in 1957. It was a book of essays on American politicians who risked their careers fighting for just but unpopular causes. The book gave him the needed mileage as a politician and won him admiration in literary and other circles.

In the 1956 Democratic Convention Kennedy failed to win the nomination for the post of Vice President under the former Illinois Governor Adlai Stevenson, who was nominated for the post of President. It was a blessing in disguise that Kennedy did not get nominated for Stevenson lost to Eisenhower in the elections.

Kennedy aspired to be nominated as a Presidential candidate for the 1960 Democratic presidential elections. He faced a number of hurdles. Many party leaders lacked confidence in him, as they considered him too young and inexperienced for the post. Many also doubted a Roman Catholic's chance to win a predominantly Protestant country. Kennedy even lacked the support of many liberals, who backed either Hubert Humphery of Minnesota or Adlai Stevenson. Kennedy proved all these apprehensions as baseless.

Kennedy won in West Virginia, that was an essentially Protestant State. Kennedy quelled the fear of Protestants that a Catholic might be subject to orders of the head of the Roman Catholic church at Rome. He made clear cut definite statements in this regard. In a speech before the Greater Houston Ministerial Association, Kennedy said, "I believe in an America where the separation of the church and state is absolute. . . . where no public official either requests or accepts instructions on public policy from. . . . (an) ecclesiastical source."

During his campaign Kennedy visited 46 states and 273 cities. His rival Republican candidate was Richard Nixon.

Kennedy proved himself to be an able debater in all the nationally televised debates. That he was too young and inexperienced was soon a discredited assumption. The support he received from the blacks in the important Northern States was a contributed to his election. The states of Illinois and Pennsylvania forwarded their full support to Kennedy because Kennedy along with his brother Robert had tried to obtain the release of the civil rights leader Martin Luther King Jr.

The election drew a record of 69 million voters to the polls, but Kennedy won only by 113,000 votes, He won 49.7% of the popular vote and Nixon won 49.6%. It was the closest popular vote in 72 years. However because Kennedy won most of the larger states in the north east U.S, he received 303 electoral votes to Nixon's 219.

Kennedy was inducted as the President of the United States on January 20, 1961. In his inaugural address Kennedy appealed for, "a new world of law, where the strong are Just and the week secure and peace preserved." Recognizing the difficulties of the goal he said, "All this will not be finished in the first hundred days. . . . Nor will it be finished in the first thousand days, nor in the life of this administration, nor even perhaps in our lifetime on this planet. But let us begin." His forthright sincerity won the hearts of people all over the nation. His hope was to bring new ideas and new methods into the executive branch. The credit of developing Kennedy into a political liberal goes to Theodore C Sorenson, a member of

Kennedy's staff since his days at the Senate. Soreson wrote many of Kennedy's speeches.

The first couple determined to make the White House the nexus of cultural activity of the nation. Writers, artists, poets, scientists and musicians were encouraged. On one occasion, the Kennedy's held a reception for all the American winners of the Noble Prize. Kennedy endowed with a good sense of humour remarked that more talent and genius was at the White House that night than there had been since Thomas Jefferson had dined alone.

Kennedy's sense of humour never waned even when his political life was beset with crises. At a meeting with the leader of the USSR, Nikita Kruschev, Kennedy asked the name of the medal Kruschev was wearing. When the premier identified it as the Lenin Peace Medal, Kennedy remarked, "I hope you keep it." On another occasion he told a group of Republican business leaders," It would be premature to ask for your support in the next election and inaccurate to thank you for it in the past."

On taking over office, Kennedy started to work arduously to get some of the bills passed in the parliament. He was quite successful in doing so. In his first year at office the Congress passed a major housing bill, a law increasing the minimum wages, and a bill granting federal aid to the economically depressed areas of the United States. The most original piece of legislation Kennedy put through Congress was the bill creating the Peace Corps, an agency that trained American volunteers to perform social and humanitarian service overseas. The programme's goal was to promote world peace and friendship with developing countries. The idea of American volunteers helping people in foreign lands touched the idealism of many citizens. Within two years, Peace Corps volunteers were working in Asia, Africa and Latin America, living with the people and working on education, public health, and agricultural projects.

The civil rights movement was at its height during Kennedy's term as President. Kennedy attempted to aid the black cause by enforcing existing laws. He particularly wanted to end discrimination in federally financed projects or in companies that were doing business with the government.

In September 1962 Governor Ross. R. Barnett of Mississippi ignored a court order and prevented James H. Meredith, a black man from enrolling at the state university. On the night of 29, even as the president went on national television to appeal to the people of Mississippi to obey the law, rioting began on the campus. After 15 hours of rioting and two deaths, Kennedy sent in troops to restore order. Meridth was admitted to the university, and troops and federal marshals remained on campus to ensure safety. There were other such instances that Kennedy handled in the same just way. Kennedy also appealed to the Congress to pass a civil rights bill that would guarantee blacks the right to vote, to attend public school, to have equal access to jobs, and to have access to public acommodation. Kennedy told the American people, "Now the time has come for this nation to fulfill its promises. . . to act, to make a commitment it has not fully made in this century to the proposition that race has no place in American life or law. "Though Kennedy began to lose popularity because of his staunch support to the civil right movement he never gave up his fight for justice.

When Cuba became communist, the Kennedy adminis-tration approved of an invasion by the Cuban exiles of America. They were trained by the Americans to invade Cuba and fight their cause. In April 1961, 1000 Cuban exiles made an amphibious landing in Cuba at a place called the Bay of Pigs. Their plan was to move inland and join the anti-Castro forces to stage a revolt simultaneously, but instead Castro's forces were there to meet the invaders. The revolt in the interior did not materialise, and air support, promised by the CIA never came. The exiles were defeated and taken prisoners. Castro demanded money for their release. Kennedy refused to negotiate with Castro, but he took steps to encourage both business and private citizens to reach an agreement with Castro and to contribute to their ransom. On December 25, 1962, 1113 prisoners were released with in exchange for food and medical supplies valued at a total of approximately $53 million.

The Cuban Missile Crisis was perhaps the world's closest approach to nuclear war. In 1960 Soviet Premier Krushchev decided to supply Cuba with nuclear missiles that would put an end to the eastern United States within range of nuclear missile attack. Krushchev when asked denied that any missiles were being supplied to Cuba, but in the summer of 1962 US spy planes flying over Cuba photographed Soviet -managed construction work and spotted the first missile on October 14.

Kennedy in response to this discovery called upon Krushchev, "to halt and eliminate this clandestine, reckless and provocative threat to the world peace and to stable relations between the two nations." Kennedy did not budge from his stance until the nuclear base at Cuba was dismantled. Kennedy did not succeed in Vietnam as well.

On November 22, 1963, President and Mrs. Kennedy were in Dallas, Texas, trying to win support in a state that Kennedy had barely carried in 1960. They were sitting at the head of a motorcade in an open convertible waving to the crowds when two bullents were shot in rapid succession . One bullet pierced the head of the President who fell forward in a pool of blood. Midst screams, hysteria and wailing he was rushed to the Parkland Hospital where he was pronounced dead. The bullets that killed the president were fired from the sixth story window of a near by house. That afternoon, Lee Harvey Oswald, who was employed at the warehouse was arrested in Dallas movie theater and charged with murder. Two days later as the suspect was being transferred from one jail to another, the Dallas nightclub owner Jack Ruby sprang out from a group of reporters and as millions watched on television, fired a revolver into Oswald's left side. Oswald died in the same hospital where the late president had breathed his last.

The world was shocked at the brutal and sudden way in which their charismatic president was taken away from them. Less than two hours after the shooting, aboard the presidential plane at the Dallas airport, Lyndon B. Johnson was sworn in as the 36th President of the United States. Kennedy was buried at the Arlington National Cemetery after a state funeral which was attended by delegates from 92 nations.

Keeping the family tradition Robert Kennedy aspired to the nomination as the candidate for the Democratic Presidential seat in 1968. He was shot dead on 6th June 1968 by an Arab assassin. His brother Edward stepped into his shoes and went on to become a Senator. The Kennedy's kept their promise.

Mao Tse -Tung

The credit of establishing The People's Republic of China after a hard bitter struggle of twenty five years goes to Mao Tse-tung . A visionary, a guerrilla leader, a philosopher Mao's revolution of 700 million Chinese left the world dumfounded as the largest communist state in the world came into being and Mao became the chairman of the Communist Party of China at the age of 54. Challenging the USSR's orthodoxy, Mao strayed from the Soviet Marxist model. He attempted to build a socialist society based on peasant farming rather than on a centralized, bureaucatic, industrlized economy. He believed that humility and hardwork went hand in hand and in a speech to the party congress in 1956, he said, "Even though we have attained extraordinary great achievements, there is no reason to be arrogant. Modesty makes you move forward, arrogance makes you go backwards. I should always remember this truth. "He also believed in the need to continually strive for progress and never to let complacency take over. That was the secret to success.

Mao belonged to the peasant class. His childhood exposed him to the hard life of the peasants, but it also made him aware of the dormant strength that the peasant population possessed. They could be the influencing factor in any decision by virtue of sheer population, Mao realized this. He saw the tremendous source of energy the peasants possessed and came to the conclusion that it only needed to be tapped and channelised. It would he had no doubt about it, reap great results. And it did.

Mao was born on 26 December, 1893, in the village of Shaoshan, Hunan province. Carrying manure for his father's field did not interest Mao. Instead, China's history fascinated young Mao. During his long sojourns in the world of books he came in contact with the great Taiping rebellion where the peasants rising in rebellion had tried to form a communist community of sorts. They had been inspired by Christianity but were suppressed by the Manchus. He also read of the legendary Sun-Yat Sen who overthrowing the Manchu dynasty founded the republic of China. His readings made him more than ever determined to do something for the peasants of China.

To obtain an education Mao had to struggle against the iron will of his father who thought education was futile and who could not spare him from the daily chores of farming. But Mao struggled, borrowed money from his friends and attended school whenever he could. He joined a library at Changsha and devoured all the books and periodicals there. From dawn to dusk he poured over the written word and tried to satisfy his insatiable appetite. He graduated from the Chansha's teacher's training school in 1918.

During the 1911-1912 revolution against the Manchu dynasty he served briefly in the Nationalist army . He worked as a library assistant in the Beijing University when the anti Japanese Fourth of May movement began. He returned to Changsha in 1920 as head of a primary school. Here his attempts to organize mass education were suppressed. By this time he was very much influenced by Marxist thought. On reading the Communist Manifesto in 1920 Mao said, "I had become in theory and to some extent in action a Marxist."

Mao married the daughter of his old tutor, Yang Kai-hui. She too like him was a Communist and was executed in Shanghai in 1930. In May 1921 Mao went to Shanghai and founded together with the others the Chinese Communist Party. He became a full time party worker. By the time he was thirty three he was acting Director of the Kuomintang Propaganda Department and also Director of the National Peasant Movement Institute which was the chief center for training cadres of peasants.

In the meanwhile in 1925 Dr SunYat -sen died . Chaing Kai-Shek succeeded him. As a result of the agreement between the Russian Bolsheviks and SunYat-Sen's Kuomintang, a combined front was formed with the Communists. Under Chaing Kai-Shek soon differences cropped up with the Communists who were not being taken into the complete confidence and were alienated from the directives given from the Communist international at Moscow. Friction also increased between the right wing of the Kuomingtang, that was backed by the landlords and Communists. The Kuomingtang were suspicious of the Communist plans for the peasant land reforms.

In early 1927, mao wrote Report of . . . . the Peasant Movement in Hunan, after witnessing a rising of impoverished peasants in his home province. In it he argued that the peasant discontent was the major force in China and deserved

Communist support. His advice was rejected because the Moscow-based Cimintern wanted to maintain Communist alliance with the Nationalists under Chiang Kai-Shek. Kuomingtang forces suppressed an "Autumn Harvest" an uprising of peasants, a remnant of which Mao led to safety in the mountains of Jiangxi (Kiangsi). Chaing promptly dismantled the Kuomingtang grass-roots organizations, suspecting Communist infiltration, while Mao, in Jiangxi, continued to exert Communist influence over the peasants. The result was that, in a country where village power was critical, the Communists gained the advantage.

In the snow covered mountains of Chingkangshan Mao displayed great qualities of leadership. He motivated about a thousand peasants into communist thinking. He set up a soviet government and mobilized the First Red Army. In May 1928, he was encouraged and aided by the arrival of Chu the from Nanchang. The govt. of Stalin recognized Mao's contribution to Communism and he reinstated Mao in the Central Committee and in the Politburo at the Sixth Congress of the Communist Party held at Moscow. The Kuomingtang army under Chaing Kai-Shek however continued in its effort to disrupt and destroy the activities of the Communists. Between December 1930 and October 1933 he sent large armies against the Communists only to incur repeated defeats. Mao's guerrilla tactics and Chu Teh's disciplined army and the unconditional support of the local peasants were causes for the defeat the Kuomingtang army. But Chiang Kai-Shek's fifth campaign proved difficult for the Communists. They were forced to break out of the Kiangsi mountains. They decided to move the north west province of Shensi and Kansu near the great wall of China. But their move was not going to be easy and had to carefully planned. A-part from the threat posed by the Kuomingtang army they were aware of the Japanese threat from the north-east.

In October 1934, Mao began the long march of the communist army towards the great wall of China. In route the soldiers not only had to combat the Kuomingtang army but the local tribes, flooded rivers, swampy grasslands and the hazardous snow capped mountains. It was one of the bravest marches recorded in modern history. They reached Shensi in October 1935.

At Shensi they trained local recruits, taught the local peasants, set up soviets and collected information on Japanese movements and the latest developments of the Kuomingtang army. Chiang Kai-Shek had become a Generalissimo of the Kuomingtang armies and the chairman of the Executive Yuan.

The arrest of Chiang Kai-Shek at Sian proved to the turning point in history. Instead of having him executed as the other Communists desired Mao impressed upon the Genneralissimo to co-operate against the Japanese. The Japanese were defeated and on October 1st 1949, the Central People's Government was established at Peking. Mao Tse-Tung was appointed the Chaiman of the largest Communist state in the world.

At first Mao followed the Soviet model for constructing a socialist society through redistribution of land, heavy industrialization, and centralized bureaucracy. But during the years in Shaanxi he had evolved an alternative that reflected China's demography, his own experience with the pesants and his hostility to bureaucracy. Economically he stressed self-reliance through labour-intensive rather than technologically advanced cooperative agriculture and through local community effort. Politically he created the concept of "mass-line" leadership, which integrated intellectuals with peasant guerrilla leaders as a fundamental economic and social strategy.

In 1956 his slogan "let a hundred flowers bloom, let diverse schools of thought contend" was a reaction to the Soviet condemnation of Stalin. It was intended to conciliate intellectuals by allowing them to criticize bureaocracy. His speech, "On the Ten Great Relationships" rejected Soviet emphasis on heavy industry, arguing that increasing peasant purchasing power was the key to rapid socialist and economic development. His 1957 speech "On correct handling of Contradictions among the People," repudiated the Soviet denial of contradictions in a socialist society, insisting that conflict was both inevitable and healthy.

In 1958 he applied his policies in the Great Leap Forward. This attempted to substitute the bureaucratic state with a cellular system of local communes and projects united by a common ideology. The Great Leap failed and the Communists returned to the East European practice of giving autonomy to large undertakings, supressing small ones and being led by a handful of educated elite. Though Mao retired he never let go of his belief that the maximum participation was the only route to true socialism. In the Great Proletarian Cultural Revolution(1966-69) he mobilized youth into the Red Guard to attack the party establishment. After much rioting and near destruction of the party, he allowed the army to restore order and the party to be rebuilt. He was made Supreme Commander of China in 1970. His book "The Thoughts of Chairman Mao" is widely read. He died in Beijing on September 9, 1976.

Agnes Smedly's observation of Mao perhaps best sums up this communist chief's character. In her book Battle Hymn of China she wrote, ". . . he was stubborn as a mule and a steel rod of pride and determination ran through his nature. I had the impression that he would wait and watch for years but eventually have his way."

Martin Luther King Jr.

The crusade that started against inequality during Lincoln's time reached a feverish pitch under the leadership of Martin Luther King Jr., a black American clergyman and a Noble Prize winner in the 19 fifty's. With conviction King carried the baton of non violence and fought against racism that had infected the very sinews of social thought in the United States of America. With the magic of rhetoric that is born out of pure conviction King mesmerized audiences across the nation and steadily began to carve a niche in the hearts of the whites who becoming aware of their prejudice decided to do away with it. In the long history of the civil rights movement in America the contribution of Martin Luther King reigns supreme.

King was the eldest son of Martin Luther King Sr. a Baptist minister and his wife Alberta King. King's father was a pastor of a large Atlanta church, Ebenezer Baptist. This church had been founded by King's maternal grandfather.

King was born in Atlanta, Georgia in 1929. Racisim was the accepted order of the day when King started to attend school. He attended a segregated school as was the form . He excelled there. He graduated from Morehouse College at the age of 15 with a bachelor's degree in sociology. Here he sharpened his rhetoric skills and became a much acclaimed debator. He then attended the Crozer Theological Seminary in Pennsylvania and graduated from there in 1951. Here too he received admiration for his public speaking abilities. He was by far the most effective speaker the college had seen in many years. From Boston University he received a doctoral degree in systematic theology in 1955.

King's ecclesiastical background nurtured in him a firm faith that all men are created equal and evoked in him a desire to see that justice is done. A highly moral soul he never steered from the path of non violence even a fraction to achieve his aim. In God's Kingdom justice must be done, he believed but -only peacefully. King was influenced by protest leaders like Mahatma Gandhi who believed that the only true way to freedom was through non-violence. Benjamin E. Mays, president of Morehouse and a leader in the national community of racially liberal clergymen, was specially important in shaping King's theological development. The strength of mind that comes with practice of self control is what made King successful in paving a path ridden with prejudice and racial contempt.

In 1953 King married Coretta Scott, a music student and a native of Alabama. In 1954 King accepted his first pastorate at the Dexter Avenue Baptist Church in Montogomery, Alabama. The church had a well-educated congregation and had been recently led by a minister who had protested against segregation.

King's appointment at Montgomery rushed him into the thick of action. The Montgomery blacks had been seething against mistreatment of blacks in the community buses. A black was, according to segregation laws supposed to ride only in the back of the bus and in case of a crowded bus he was to empty his seat to a white passenger. The blacks under the local branch of the National Association for the Advancement of Coloured People (NAACP) decided to challenge these unjust laws. On December 1, 1955, Rosa Parks, a leading member of the NAACP, was ordered by a bus driver to give up her seat . When she refused she was arrested and taken to jail. Local leaders of the NAACP recognized the potency of the situation and saw it as a good opportunity to rake up the issue so it receives some attention. The time, Nixon believed was ripe for protest. King a relative new comer in the Montgomery black community was chosen to lead the protest. He had no enemies and his powerful public speaking was an asset not to be ignored. It gave a roaring impetus to the civil right movement that was soon to take on national dimension.

King was chosen as the president of the Montgomery Improvement association (MIA). Under his leadership the MIA directed the bus boycott. The boycott lasted for more than a year. King's memoir of the bus boycott, Stride Towards Freedom, provided a thoughtful account of the intrinsic dreams and desires that the blacks endeavored to fulfill. It demonstrated a new spirit of protest among Southern blacks. King's serious demeanor and consistent appeal to Christian brotherhood and American idealism made a positive impression on the whites outside the South. King, along with all that he was associated with began to get international attention. Incidents of violence against black protesters, including bombing of King's home focused media attention on Montgomery.

In 1956 an attorney for the MIA filed a lawsuit in federal court seeking an injunction against Montgomery's segregated seating practices. The federal court ruled in favour of the MIA, ordering the city's buses to be desegregated. The city government appealed the ruling to the United States Supreme Court. The Supreme Court upheld the decision of the lower court. King was a national figure in the civil rights movement.

King's life from then on was targeted at ending these awful practices that under the guise of law had so invaded the social strata of society. His fight was against injustice and his dedication to the cause was total. In 1957 King helped found the Southern Christian Leadership Conference (SCLC), an organization of black churches and ministers that aimed to challenge racial segregation. King was appointed the president of the SCLC. He organized fund raising during his preaching tours in the Northern Churches.

King along with the SCLC tried to legally fight the racists injustice in court. Their method of protest was always nonviolent. But their demonstrations so infuriated the whites that they reacted violently. This further promoted their cause and eventually forced the federal government to confront issues of injustice and racism in the South.

King's success was mainly due to the support he received from the North. Jewish activist and black civil right activists closely worked with King planning new strategies to destroy segregation. Many from the Jewish communities aided the movement by providing monetary aid. Bayard Rustin, a black civil rights and peace activist and Stanley Levison, a Jewish activist and former member of the American Communist Party were prime in the help they rendered to King.

King visited India and tried to emulate in totality the essence of Gandhi's Satyagraha - the principle of nonviolent persusion. This was the to be his main method of protest. The next year he gave up his pastorate in Montgomery and became a co-pastor (with his father) of the Ebenezer Baptist Church in Atlanta.

In 1961 in Albany, Georgia, the SCLC joined local demonstrations against segregated restaurants, hotels, transit and housing. The demonstrations were large and annoyed the white officials who rounded up hundreds of demonstrators in jail and the blacks ran out of money to bail out their people. The effort ended in a fiasco.

In Alabama the strategy of the SCLC to create a lot of dissent and disorder in the state due to its intensive demonstrations was met with succession May 1963 teenagers and children also joined the demonstrations on the streets of Birmingham. The sheer number of protesters angered the police commissioner, Eugene "Bull" Connor. Police officers with attack dogs and firefighters with high pressure water hoses were sent against the marches. This act of brutish violence on the part of the Birmingham police caught the eye of the media who gave unsavory publicity to the police. The national reaction to the violence was acute and helped to build support for the black civil right movement. During the demonstration King was arrested and he wrote the famous "Letter from the Birmingham City Jail. "In this he argued that individuals had a moral right to disobey unjust laws. King was acclaimed as the new national moral leader and his personality encouraged many Americans to support the national legislation against segregation.

On August 28, 1963, king delivered the keynote address to an audience of more than 200,000 civil right supporters. His "I Have a Dream" speech expressed the hopes of the civil rights movement in oratory as moving as any in American history:I have a dream that one day this nation will rise up and live out the true meaning of its creed: 'We hold these truths to be self-evident, that all men are created equal'.... I have a dream that my four children will one day live in a nation where they will not be judged by the colour of their skin but by the content of their character. "This speech in the backdrop of the demonstrations at Birmingham created the political momentum that resulted in the passing of the Civil Rights Act in 1964. This act prohibited segregation in public accomodations, as well as discrimination in education and empolyment. King's peaceful protests and his exemplary moral stance on all the civil rights issues won him the Nobel Prize for Peace in 1964.

King next goal was to procure for the blacks voting rights in the state. In 1965 the SCLC joined a voting-rights protest march that was planned to go from Selma, Alabama, to the state capital of Montgomery, more than 80 kms away. The police met the marchers aggressively and in the face of all media attention they tear-gassed the protestors. It resulted in violence and bloodshed. The day was known as Bloody Sunday. It resulted in the federal court's ruling to ban police interference and the march was once again resumed two weeks later. At Montgomery King addressed a rally of 20, 000 people in front of the capitol building. The Voting Rights Act was signed by President Lyndon Johnson in 1965. The act suspended the use of tests and other voter qualification tests that often have been used to prevent blacks from registering to vote.

King soon turned his attention to the economic difficulties faced by the Black community in the North. In 1967 he began planning a Poor People's Campaign to pressure the national lawmakers to address the issue of economic justice.

King's tireless dedication to the black cause that brought him fame and renown also brought him to door's death. In Memphis while supporting the rights of the black garbage workers he was shot by a sniper on 4 August 1968. James Earl Ray an escaped convict pleaded guilty to the murder of King and was sentenced to 99 years of prison.

King's assassination triggered riots in about a 100 states of the United States. The country had lost not only a dynamic leader of the blacks but a moral consciousness that made everyone stop and think awile. His booming resonating voice that had so stirred many a soul was muted forever. It would live on only in the minds of the people who were fortunate enough to be part in the making of history with Martin Luther King Jr.

Today's America can boast of realizing King's "dream". It stands on the steadfast principle of liberty, equality and fraternity. In a moving tribute to the champion of justice the Congress of the United States in 1983 designated a national holiday in King's honour that is observed nation wide on the third Monday in January. This is a day that falls on or near King's birthday on January 15.

Pablo Picasso

The name of Picasso is associated with the greatest art that the 20th century ever saw. A painter and a sculptor, Picasso was a unique inventor of forms and styles. Blessed with that inner vision that only a creative mind can see Picasso's plethora of work penetrated all walks of life. Adding that extra fillip of imagination he created beauty that has been immortalized in more than 20,000 works.

Born in Malaga Spain on 25 October 1881, Picasso was the son of Jose Ruiz Blasco, an art teacher, and Maria Picassoy Lopez. The world would never have known Pablo Picasso if his uncle Don Salvodor's presence of mind had not saved him. Picasso on birth was thought to have been a still born and abandoned on the table. His uncle rushed him to the doctor and saved the child of dying of asphyxia. The world of art is indebted to this good stroke of luck that saved the greatest artist of the century.

Picasso's genius manifested early. As a mere child he would sit for hours with a pencil and paper drawing to his hearts content. The Malagna beeches were also a favourite spot for his creative expressions. At the age of 10 he made his first paintings and at 15 he performed brilliantly in the entrance exam at the Barcelona School of Fine Art. His large academic canvas Science and Charity depicting a doctor, a nun, and a child at a sick woman's bedside, won a gold medal. Until 1898 Picasso always used his father's name, Ruiz, and his mother's name Picasso to sign his pictures. After about 1901 he dropped "Ruiz" and used only Picasso to sign his pictures.

Picasso's father was forced to move to Corunna and teach at a secondary school there. It was a blow and an insult. Don Jose became more and difficult to handle. It was only on restoring his lost prestige when he got a job at the prestigious Barcelona School of Fine Arts that Don Jose's restored his good humour. The exposure at the Barcelona School of fine Art put Picasso on the road to earnest painting. In these early days he was influenced by Daumier, Van Gogh and Toulouse-Lautrec. He then joined the Royal Academy of San Fernando at Madrid where he astonished every one with his brilliant performance. His genius was instantly recognised. He returned to Barcelona only to move to Paris in 1904 where the city's Bohemian lifestyle appealed to his young iconoclastic ideas.

Picasso found the city's bohemian life facinating. He tried to capture each nuance of the life that so invigorated his senses. Influenenced by the postimpressionism of Paul Gauguin he captured people in dance halls and cafe's. He was even influenced by symbolist painters called the Nabis. The themes of the French painters Edgar Degas and Henri de Toulouse-Lautrec exerted a strong influence on Picasso's work. Picasso's Blue Room (1901) reflects the work of both these painters and at the same time shows evolution towards the Blue Period, so called because various shades of blue dominated his work for the next few years. His painting expressed human misery. Blind figures, beggars, alchoholics and prostitutes were subjects of his paintings which bore the mark of Spanish artist El Greco.

During these early years in Paris Picasso held many exhibitions of his work. In 1912 a group of his Cubist paintings were shown at the Stradfford Gallery in London. The prices 2 Pounds to 20 Pounds! The price of a painting of the same period today is 75,000 Pounds!

Picasso's frequent exhibitions earned him an international reputation. His genius was versitille. Not only did his paintings gain acclaim but his sculptures and his designer costumes also received praise. In the field of visual art he was the master. Cubism, Expressionism, Surrealism; sculpture, ceramics, stage decor and costume design; the arts of collage and poster design; of etching and book illustration he was master of them all. One can count Picasso's genius only next to Leonardo da Vinci's. He designed costumes for the Diaghileff Russian ballet . He later married a ballerina Olga Koklova in 1918 in Spain. They returned to Picasso's beloved Paris in the aftermath of the war only to discover the deep scars that World War I had left. His cherished friend Apollinaire who had been severely wounded in the head died after a few days of his return. Picasso received the news at the time when he was painting a self portrait. So shocked and grieved was he that his friend's death marked an end to an era of painting. Picasso never did make a self portrait again.

Much of Picasso's life in France was spent near the sea. He bought the seventeenth century Chateau du Boisegeloup near Paris in 1932. But his marriage was running into difficulty. He had also met Marie Therese Walter a new and beautiful model. This further created a rift between the husband and wife and they soon parted. Marie was Picasso's latest love and posed as a model for many of his paintings during this period. In harmonious curvilinear lines he expressed underlying eroticism in paintings such as Girl Before a Mirror. In 1935 Picasso made the etching Minotauromachy, a major work combining minotaur and bullfight themes. It presupposes the famous Guernica, the master piece of the twentieth century.

A thorough bred Spaniard at heart Picasso was outraged at the Spanish dictator, Francisco Franco's bombardment of the Basque town of Guernica on April 26, 1937 during the Spanish civil war. He was moved to paint the colossal mural

Guernica that was hung in the Spanish Pavilion of the Paris International Exposition of 1937. Picasso employed imagery to express his outrage. The bull, the dying horse, a fallen warrior, a mother and dead child, a woman trapped in a burning building, another rushing into the scene and a figure leaning from a window and holding a lamp all went on to portray the anguish of the Spanish people. It is the single most prized possession twentieth century can boast of. Apart from the striking accuracy of the imagery it celebrates man's deepest agony in face of baseless inhumanity.

After the Spanish Civil war ended Picasso was unable to return to his native land. He joined the French Communist party to show his support to France to whom he was much indebted . In a statement he said, "My adhesion to the Communist Party is the logical outcome of my whole life. . . I was so anxious to find a homeland again, I have always been in exile, now I am one no longer;until Spain can at last welcome me back, the French Communist Party has opened its arms to me. "Picasso in the aftermath of the war continued to attend communist meetings and evolved the symbol of peace (a lithograph of a white dove) which was accorded international acceptance. Today it is a universal symbol of peace and it reiterates Picasso's belief who said, "I stand for life against death; I stand for peace against war."

In 1954 he met a beautiful young girl Jacqueline Roque who became his second wife. He painted and lithographed a series of paintings of her that became world famous. Picasso made important sculptures during this time: *Man with Sleep*, an over life size bronze, emanates peace and hope, and She-Goat a bronze cast from an assemblage of flowerpots, a wicker basket, and other diverse materials. In 1964 Picasso completed a welded *maquette* for the 18.3 m sculpture *Head of a Woman*, for Chicago's Civic Center. In 1968 during a seven month period he created an amazing series of 347 engravings, restating earlier themes.

The boundless energy of this little sun burned man with compelling black eyes that saw beyond the surface into the scheme of things came to an end on April 8, 1973. He was reputed to be worth between five to six hundred million pounds.

Catherine The Great Empress Of Russia

In a totally patriarchal setup when the concept of feminism was still unknown to the world Catherine II of Russia ruled the Russian empire from 1762-96. Her laudable work of westernization of the Russian empire and her reforms of the underdog earned her the cognomen of "Great." She shaped the destiny of Russia in an undeniable way.

Catherine II was born Sophie Fredricke von Anhalt-Zerbst. She was born in Stettin (now Szczecin, Poland) on May 2, 1929, the daughter of a minor German prince. At the age of fourteen she arrived in Russia on the invitation of the Empress

Elizabeth of Russia as a prospective bride for her nephew Grand Duke Peter. On her arrival at Moscow, little did this German born girl know that her future destiny was to be Russia's destiny. She was accepted as the bride to be of the Grand Duke Peter.

Sophie's introduction to her prospective husband was far from happy. She was faced with a debauched young man of sixteen years of age who openly declared his lack of interest in her and publicly claimed his interest in his aunt's maid of honour Elizabeth Vorontzov. But things had been arranged by the monarchy and there was no turning back on royal arrangements. The Empress had decided Sophie's fate. Soon Sophie was being tutored in the Russian language. She was converted to the Greek Church and received the name of Catherine Alexeyevna, in the Russian tradition. But during her training Sophie discovered her passion for all things Russian. It was a spontaneous attraction to the culture, language and the general Russian ethos and had nothing to do with the coercion of the Empress. If her oncoming marriage was a dreaded event, her newly discovered love of Russia was her salvation. It was ultimately this that put her, a German, on the path of winning the Russians and becoming the beloved Empress of the Russian people. In August 1745 she was bethroed to Peter and was married to him at the age of sixteen.

As expected the conjugal relationship did not bring any happiness to Catherine. Her boorish husband under the autocratic reign of the empress isolated her life. The finery of the French lifestyle by which she had been brought up had become a distant past. Her loneliness forced her to take to extramarital affairs that became numerous as the years went by. But neither her husband nor the empress cared much for her, to object to these liasons. Catherine continued in the same tradition and years rolled by. She in the meanwhile had given birth to her two children—a son Paul and a daughter, both of whom were not believed to be Peter's. The children at birth were taken away by the Empress to be brought up by her and Catherine was once again left to her amorous persuits. In January 1762 the Empress died and Catherine's husband becoming the Czar became Peter III of Russia.

Peter at the time was still in love with Elizabeth Vorontzov. Catherine saw her as a dangerous rival. But she also knew the unpopularity that Peter suffered. Peter had declared quite openly his love for all things German. So smitten was he by the German mania that his allegiance to Fredrick the Great of Prussia was quite a well accepted public truth. The Russians naturally began to hate this Russian and were more and more inclined towards this German princess who had made Russia her own in every way possible. Gregory Orlov, Catherine's lover appealed to the army to support Catherine whose life was seen to be in danger. Peter had threatened her with arrest and divorce. Peter drove off to his palace with his mistress at Oranienbaum on May 22, 1762. That was the last he saw of his empire for his public abandonment of his wife and his pro German stance made the people of Russia swear by Catherine's name. "Long live the Empress Catherine," was a slogan echoed in each battalion of the Russian Army. Peter was subsequently arrested and was imprisoned at Ropscha. He later died, it is said a victim of colic but the mystery surrounding his death remains. Catherine became the Empress of Russia.

Catherine's astute mind and an educated French background made her an able ruler. She was acquainted with the literature of the French Enlightenment and it moulded her political thinking. She corresponded extensively with Voltaire and Denis Diderot and gave them financial support whenever needed. She aimed at creating a favouable impression of Russia in the foreign lands. She tried to cultivate an educated atmosphere in her court, where wine and plain debauchery were no longer the ethos. To Catherine goes the credit of establishing the first Russian school for girls and a medical college to provide health care for her subjects.

In 1766 Catherine published her Instructions which limited the powers of the nobles and the landowners over the serfs. This was greatly opposed. Catherine had to bow to the wishes of the rich class She tried to win the support of a small section of the Russian gentry. She confirmed Peter III's emancipation of the gentry from compulsory military service, granted them many other privileges, and showered her supporters with titles, offices, state lands, and serfs to work in their fields. Thus though she genuinely hated serfdom the circumstances coerced her in such a way that the plight of the serfs became more miserable than before. This resulted in a revolt of the peasants under a Cossack named Pugachev in 1773. The revolt was quelled and Pugachev was executed. The cossack army was disbanded and other Cossacks were granted special privileges in an effort to transform them into loyal supporters of the autocracy.

In 1775, Catherine issued the "Statute of Provinces" This provided for local administration and provincial self-government and it set up a local regular judiciary. This continued till the latter half of the nineteenth century.

The territory of the Russian empire greatly expanded under the sagacious rule of Catherine. In 1768 in alliance with Frederick the Great of Prussia, Catherine invaded the Turks and the Austrians. The war lasted six years and Catherine had gained a territory in the south for Russia. In 1787 Catherine allied with Austria against Turkey and Prussia to gain more land. As a result of her two wars with the Ottoman empire and the annexation of Crimea, Russia gained control of the northern coast of the Black Sea. Russian control over Poland-Lithuania was also greatly extended, culminating in the annexation of large tracts of territory in the three portions of Poland(1772, 1793, 1795).

Under the mantle of the tough empress Catherine remained essentially a feminine woman attracting men by her wit, charm and power. She continued to have liaisons with many but her personal involvement never deterred her from her aim at promoting Russia and doing the best for her welfare. Though not attached to her son Paul whom she kept in subjection, she was very fond of her grandchildren. She arranged the marriage of her grand daughter Alexandrina with King Gustavus Adolphus of Sweden. But the young King on reading the marriage contract refused to sign it as Catherine had inserted many articles not to his liking. It was the biggest blow that her highness recived. A rush of blood on receiving the news only a prognosis of what was to come. On November 10, 1796, a few weeks later she died of apoplexy.

The loss of this great empress was felt throughout Russia. The country mourned and history took note of this great lady who carved a story of success from what might have been fragments of disillusion to begin with. In the latter half of the nineteenth century at the palace a guard still stood posted in the middle of the lawn by an order of Catherine the Great nearly a century before. It was, according to legend to prevent anyone from picking the first flower of the season from the frozen ground. Her keen eye for detail is just one of the many reasons that made this lady a success in the autocratic world of men.

Adolf Hitler

On 30th April 1945 Adolf Hitler the greatest dictator and tyrant of the century committed suicide in his Berlin bunker after Germany lost the war. The news rocked the headlines all over the world. Nations across the globe were shocked but no one mourned. Hitler's end was the end of an era of racism and hatred that had corroded the very foundation of civilization. Germany under Hitler's regime fully terrorized the world with its military might and unjust anti sometism operations. The holocaust of the Jews by Hitler in the gas chambers and extermination camps left the world astonished at such rampant cruelty that paraded recklessly under Hitler's dictatorship.

Adolf Hitler was born in 1889 at Braunau in Austria. His father was a minor custom's official and his mother a peasant girl. At school Hitler was a poor student and he never completed high school. His heart was set on painting and because of want of talent he failed to get admission in the Academy of Fine Arts in Vienna, though he applied twice. He lived in Vienna on a shoe string budget and passed his time painting second rate postcards. He developed a passion for politics. His favourite haunt became night shelters that gossiped over free soup and politics. Hitler had no other passion. Wine, women and wealth held no attraction for this young man. Hitler soon became acquainted with power for the first time and this lust for power was to seduce him and put him on the path of mass annihilation some years later. The years at Vienna afforded him time to read and it is through these readings he developed anti democratic and anti-Jewish convictions. A keen admiration for the outstanding individual and a contempt for the masses such became his philosophy. These strains of thought took further shape when he got permission from King Ludwig III of Bavaria to join the German army in World War I.

Hitler distinguished himself as a soldier during the World War I and he won the Iron Cross. But no record exists as to what he won the cross for. His sense of commitment to the war was almost fanatic, so recalled his fellow soldiers. The obsession with war set him apart from the others. Anti Jewish sentiments became stronger and the pro German stance well ingrained. Hitler began to believe in the superiority of the Aryan race and would often spend hours haranguing his fellow soldiers on the subject. His eccentric style left a lasting impression on all those who came in contact with him during those early days. People could not easily forget his piercing eyes that arrested the beholder in an uncanny hypnotic glare. This psychological mass hypnosis was what was responsible for Hitler's rise in power later on.

Hitler joined the political department of the German Army in Munich after the war. He founded the National Socialist Party. It consisted of various patriotic groups of men and ex soldiers. They were an active band of revolutionary and counter revolutionary plotting that ultimately challenged the Bavarian government under Ludendroff. Hitler continued to spread his gospel of racial hatred and contempt of democracy. He believed in Darwin's theory of survival of the fittest to an extreme degree. the weak must be annihilated and had no right to survive. He organized meetings, and terrorized political foes with his personal bodyguard force, the Sturmabteilung (SA, or Storm Troopers). He soon became a key figure in Bavarian politics, aided by high officials and bussinessmen. In November 1923, a time of political and economic chaos, he led an uprising (Putsch) in Munich against the postwar Weimar Republic, proclaiming himself chancellor of a new authoritarian regime. Without military support however the Putsch collapsed. As a leader of the plot Hitler was sentenced to five years imprisonment and served nine months. In jail he dictated his autobiography Mein Kampf (My Struggle). It was a semi educated attempt at putting down his thoughts that had little substance in it. The book dealt more with Hitler's future plans.

The failure of the uprising taught Hitler that the Nazi Party must use legal means to assume power. Released as a result of general amnesty in December 1924 he rebuilt his party without interference from those whose government he tried to overthrow. When the Great Depression struck in 1929, he explained it as an Jewish-Communist plot, an explanation accepted by many German's. Promising a strong Germany, jobs, and national glory he attracted millions of voters. Nazi representation in the Reichstag (parliament) rose from 12 seats in 1928 to 107 in 1930.

Hitler used the dark forces of German nationalism unsparingly. During the following two years the party kept expanding, benefiting from fear of growing unemployment, fear of Communism. Hitler's self certainty and the diffidence of his political rivals finally placed him as the Chancellor of the Reich in January 1933.

Once in power Hitler's amoral rootlessness made him the dictator of Germany where his mere whim became the law of the land. He looked at his fellow humans as mere bricks in the world structure that he wished to erect. Hitler's regime on taking charge passed the Enabling Act that permitted Hitler's government to make laws without the legislature. The Nazi domination began. Without the moderating power of the legislature Hitler's Nazi party went rampant in establishing their influence in all sectors of the German life. The bureaucracy, the judiciary the labour unions, the economy, the media cultural activities, all bore the Nazi stamp. An individual's livelihood became dependent on his or her political loyalty. Thousands of anti Nazis were taken to concentration camps and all signs of dissent were suppressed.

Completing the work of unification stated by Bismark Hitler in February 1934, made the governments of the States of Germany completely subordinate to the Reich. Hundereds of followers of the Nazi Party were summarily shot in order to purge the party of semi of anti loyalists. Hitler relied heavily on the secret police, the Gestapo, and on jails and camps to intimidate his opponents. His armament drive wiped out unemployment . He discredited the churches with charges of corruption and immorality and imposed the Nazi code on them.

Hitler's foreign success impressed the German people who by then believed in the racial superiority of the Aryan race of which Hitler claimed Germans were the highest form. His acute sense of reality and his ability to take risk was much admired throughout Germany. He reoccupied the Rhineland in March 1936. When the Spanish Civil War began in July 1936,

Hitler supported Nationalist leader Francisco Franco, supplying airplanes and weapons. German aid to Franco gave Hitler the opportunity to test his strategies and weapons technology. In October 1936 Hitler signed a pact with Italy's Fascist leader Benito Mussolini. In November 1936 he signed an Anti-Comintern treaty with Japan. In 1940 Germany signed a tripartite alliance with both Italy and Japan, pledging mutual support.

In order to get Lebensraum or living space for agriculture and industry Hitler believed the Germany needed to expand. In 1938 when Hitler occupied Austria claiming Germans were being persecuted, he encountered no resistence. In September 1938, stating the Germans in the Sudentenland in Czechoslovakia were being oppressed, he encouraged them to make demands on the Czechoslovakia government that it could not fulfill. Thus Germany had an excuse for marching into Czechoslovakia. Britain and France feared the outbreak of war and agreed to the Munich Pact, which gave Sudetenland to Germany in exchange for Germany's promise not to take additional Czech territory. However by March 1939 Hitler had brought the remainder of Czechoslovakia under German control. He was actively preparing for an aggressive maneuver towards the east.

Germany signed a nonagression pact with the Union of Soviet Republics (USSR) in August 1939 and in the pact the two countries secretly divided up Poland. Having neutralized the USSR, Hitler attacked Poland in September 1939. The Poles were quickly overpowered, and their allies, the British and the French, who had declared war on Germany, would do nothing to help. In the spring of 1940 Hitler's forces overran Denmark and Norway and a few weeks later routed the Netherlands, Belgium and France. The defeat of Britain was averted by the Royal Air Force, which fended off the German Luftwaffe.

Hitler invaded the USSR in June 1941, driven by his need of land and his hatred of communism. Confident of an early victory his army did not take provisions for the winter. The Germans were almost successful in reaching Moscow and Leningrad but the Soviet army's counter attack made them powerless. The overwhelmingly large army and the entrance of the United States into the war broke the spirits of the German army. As time passed defeat became more likely. Hitler refused to surrender. In 1944 a group of German officials attempted to assassinate Hitler, but the attempt failed.

Throughout the expansion of Germany one thing that remained a constant aim was the extermination of the Jews. In 1942 Hitler met with high ranking officials of the Reich to create the final solution to the Jewish problem. The Germans began building large extermination camps to accompany the concentration camps. Six million Jews were murdered in these camps. Endless trains took millions of Jews to the camps, seriously interfering with the war effort. Hitler's ant Jewish campaign is an example of fundamentally the most cruel anti human crusade that this century has witnessed.

Hitler's suicide on April 30 1945 with his new bride and long time companion Eva Braun marked an end the bloodiest chapter recorded in modern history. No statesman had ever been in touch with the irrational forces of human nature as was Adolf Hitler. His success was mainly due to the powerful irrational feelings that his impassioned oratory evoked in the audience. Invocation of mass hysteria in the midst of a the thumping beat of drums, huge slogans massed bands and stalwart bearers presented the most conducive environment for achieving his goals.

An American journalist describing this purposefully created emotionally seductive atmosphere writes:

". . . . . *Military bands crash a gigantic salute. Then the Fuhrer rises, stands silent for an impressive moment, speaks. . . . One hour. Two hours. Four hours. The crowd hangs on his words. . . He states the most astonishing and inaccurate things. He roars; he pleads; if need be he can weep. But he never analyses discusses or argues. He affirms attacks and comforts.*"

Hitler left behind a legacy of horror that the future generations only look at with disgust and revolt. The depths of evil to which man can stoop was fully exemplified by Hitler's anti Semetic drive. The Jewish holocaust has left scars centuries will not heal and each time posterity points its finger the name of Adolf Hitler will rise shamelessly on the pages of history.

Mahatma Gandhi

"Man's subsistence at the bare subsistence level is a mark of his strength and not of his weakness. "The words ring true when applied to the father of the Indian nation Mahatma Gandhi. Clad in a home spun 'dhoti', rimmed spectacles and a walking stick, this man's infallible values and indomitable spirit took India on the road to freedom with non violence as the only baton. Unchaining India from the cloistering shackles of the British Raj, India owes its freedom largely to this 'Great Soul' (Mahan Ataman) whose ascetic personal values and selfless spirit moved a nation so large as India to freedom with a minimum bloodshed. Gandhi's exemplary lifestyle and his utter devotion to the national struggle made him a national inspiration in a land ridden with class and caste conflict.

Mohandas Karamchand Gandhi was born on October 2, 1869 at Porbandar. He was the youngest son of Kaba Gandhi, Dewan of Rajkot, by his fourth wife. At the age of 13 he was married to Kasturba. They had four sons. Gandhi at the age of 18 went to London to study law. A strict vegetarian, he found it hard at first to adjust to the robust London lifestyle. This was quite in contrast with his unorthodox conventional upbringing. To correct matters he decided to turn a 'gentleman' He bought western clothes to suit his new lifestyle. But his inner Indian self continued to remain at odds with his new outward appearance. in an illuminating moment he realized his juvenile ambition and declared ". . . if my character makes a gentleman of me, so much the better - otherwise I should forgo the ambition." He remained in England for three years and in 1891 he was called to the Bar. He remained a vegetarian throughout his stay. His refusal to join the bandwagon and retain his individuality were traits that strengthened with years and made a Mahatma of him finally.

On his return to India he found the market for lawyers low. Getting a job was tough. After much wait he received a call from a law firm in South Africa. It was on the South African soil that Gandhi's social conscience began to take shape. The unjust Indian laws that were thoroughly against the Indian 'Sammy' (Swami) were biting. The racism was acute and Gandhi's experience in the South African soil made him sympathetic to the problems of Indian workers. On a train from Durban to Pretoria, although he was holding a first class ticket he was physically thrown out of the compartment, that was only for the privileged whites. In another instance while traveling in a coach he was beaten up by the conductor because he refused to move to the back seat. While attending the magistrate's court at Durban, Gandhi was humiliated as he was ordered by the magistrate to take off his turban. Gandhi preferred to leave the court rather than be insulted.

Apart from working at the case that Gandhi had come for he found himself racist situation in South Africa. In Pretoria he made a study of the wrongs of the Indian community and addressed meetings on the subject. He was already recognized as a leader of sorts when he decided to leave South Africa for his homeland.

On the eve of his departure someone handed him a Natal newspaper, which read a report that the Natal government was about to take away the Indian franchise. At the urgent instance of friends Gandhi decided to stay on and fight for the Indian cause. A petition was worked out and presented to the Natal Legislative Assembly. It was the first parliamentary petition ever presented by the Indians in South Africa. Evoking a huge response a memorial of 10, 000 signatures was sent to Lord Ripon, the colonial secretary.

In May 1894, Gandhi founded the Natal Indian Congress. He campaigned at raising the standard of cleanliness, sanitation, housing and education among Indians of Natal. Gandhi even began to advocate dependence on soil rather than machinery. In 1896 he returned to India for six months where he gave a number of speeches on Indian condition in Natal. He wrote a pamphlet with the aim of public awareness. On his return to South Africa, Gandhi had to face severe opposition from Natal Europeans. They tried to prevent Gandhi's boat and another steamer from setting foot on Natal soil. For twenty three days the Government held the streamers in quarantine. When at last they were allowed to disembark, Gandhi was mobbed and beaten and only the intervention of the superintendent's wife saved him.

During the Boer War Gandhi implored his fellow Indians to support the British, since they still owed allegiance to the British empire. He organized an ambulance unit and worked heroically at the front.

Gandhi returned to India only to be recalled back to South Africa by friends who needed his assistance and help. In the aftermath of the Boer War under the British administration of Transvaal the position of Indians worsened. Strict colour-bar regulations and immigration laws were put into practise. A system of permits and regulations was enforced that made Indian life quite a drudgery. Gandhi started a newspaper voicing the grievances of the Indians called Indian opinion at Phoenix near Durban.

In 1906 during the Zulu Rebellion, Gandhi recruited himself as a volunteer of an Indian company of stretcher bearers for the Natal forces. He nursed the wounded Zulu's the royalists and the rebels.

In Transvaal the Government proposed to pass stringent laws to control the movements of Indians in Transvaal. The law proposed amongst other things compulsory registration of the fingerprints of every Indian adult. In September 1906, in a mass meeting at the Johannesburg, the Indians decided to resist the "Black Act" by non violent means. Thus the Satyagraha movement was born. Gandhi, along with a deputation went to England to appeal against the Black Act to the Secretary of State for India and the Secretary of State for colonies. The Black Act was disallowed but when they reached Cape Town they realized that on granting responsible government in Transvaal, it gave Transvaal the power to pass what measures they desired. The Act was passed and many Indians including Gandhi were arrested for not regestering. Gandhi reached a compromise with Smuts, by which if a majority of Indians registered voluntarily, the act would be re-appealed . General Smuts did not carry out his part of the agreement and a new act was passed prohibiting "Asiatics" from entering Transvaal. Another statement issued by the Supreme Court ruled only Christian marriages registered by the registrar legally valid in South Africa. As a form of protest under Gandhi's leadership scores of Indians got themselves arrested.

Gandhi aided and supported the Natal coalminers who were on a strike against the three pound tax which they were forced to pay at the end of their term of indenture. Gandhi led them into Transvaal and everyone of the protesters was arrested. The miners were taken back to Natal and were flogged. They were forced to resume work. Gandhi was taken to a separate prison at Bloemfontein. The Indian Viceroy was outraged and General Smuts stepped down. Following an inquiry Gandhi and his followers were released from jail. It resulted in the Indian Relief Act, which abolished the Indian grievances. Gandhi's initiation into public life had begun. He was an acclaimed leader and there was no turning back.

Gandhi returned to India and in 1916-17 led an agitation for the abolition of immigration of indentured India labour to other parts of the empire. He studied an All India agitation and the government was forced to abolish the indentured system. The oppressed peasants of the Champaran were released from the bonded labour with Gandhi's help. Satyagraha agitation made it possible. As Gandhi said, "Hence it was that an age long abuse came to an end in a few months."

Gandhi's attention was occupied with poverty and backwardness of the Indian villages. At Khaira he organized a revolt against the government assessment of their crops after a bad harvest. He met with hardly any success in this venture.

The passing of the Rowlatt Act started an agitation nation wide that turned violent after the Amritsar massacre. Though disapproving of the violence Gandhi's loyalty to the British Raj came to an end. He now desired to obtain Swaraj for India with or without the British help. He began to work at bridging the rift between the Hindus and the Muslims that the divide and rule policy of the British had encashed on. He supported the Khilafat campaign and started the Khadi movement. In April 1920 he launched the non-co-operation movement. He strove for reforms, boycott of foreign goods and removal of untouchability. These became his prime concerns. The mass burning of foreign goods on the arrival of Prince of Wales in Bombay led to violence at the Chauri Chara. Gandhi was much disturbed at the violation of the spirit of Satyagragha. He bore the guilt of the bloodshed and retired to his ashram at Sabarmati where he was arrested. He was fasting in penance at that time. Gandhi was sentenced to six years of imprisonment. Till 1924 he was at the Yervada jail at Poona and later due to illness was taken to the Poona hospital. On discharge and barely having recovered he once again took to a fast, this time on to death. He was protesting against the growing Hindu-Muslim riots.

In 1930 Gandhi started the Dandi March—a non co-operation civil disobedience movement. Gandhi and his followers marched to Dandi to make salt from the sea. It was a movement to defy the prevailing salt laws and Gandhi achieved much success. On May 5th Gandhi was arrested under the Bombay State Prisoners Regulation Act 1827, under which a person might be imprisoned for indefinite periods without a trial. His arrest brought about a nation wide agitation which resulted in the famous Irwin-Gandhi agreement. Irwin promised to withdraw repressive measures if Gandhi's Congress would suspend direct action against the British government . But soon with the issue of the rule of Ordinances Gandhi once again began to seek negotiations with Lord Wellington. He was arrested once again and this in turn resulted in a nation wide resistance.

Gandhi did commendable work in the upliftment of the untouchables. He took a fast unto death to undo Mr. Ramsay MacDonald's Communal Award. The fast was a great success and as a result of which the Poona Pact came into being. Gandhi was arrested time and again but his Satyagarha spirit never flagged.

In 1934 Gandhi resigned from the Congress as his ethical position was at odds with some of the members. But he continued to work undeterred in spirit of the Congress. He began to work tirelessly to achieve India's freedom. On August 1942 Gandhi and his followers were arrested after the upsurge of the Quit India movement. He was kept in the Aga Khan Palace in Poona. In 1943 Gandhi once again kept a fast. His deteriorating condition caused anxiety and consequently the resignation of the three members of the Viceroy Council. Gandhi continued to correspond with the Viceroy from the prison camp, protesting against the government's repressive measures. The talks with Jinnah broke down once again, as Gandhi could not convince him that his demand for a separate Muslim state was not in keeping with the true spirit of absolute freedom.

The British government under Mr. Attlee sent a mission to India to help frame a new Constitution. The Viceroy invited Pundit Nehru to form the government. Though the League representatives were included in the Cabinet, there were riots in East Bengal, Bihar, Punjab and New Frontier Province. Gandhi went on a village to village tour to restore confidence and to spread the message of brotherhood. During the Indo-Pak discussions, Gandhi continued to visit the riot affected areas and tried to instill confidence and goodwill amongst the people. In 1948 Gandhi took another fast as a peace offering to the people of Pakistan. He was 78. The fast ended after 5 days . India rejoiced. But a small section of Indians felt that Gandhi's softening to the Muslims was a breach, a treason . Two attempts were made on his life. On January 30, 1948 the Mahatma was shot dead by Nathu Ram Godse.

The Saint of Sabarmati died a martyr's death, praying for peace amongst all communities. The nation was plunged in sorrow at the snatching away of an apostle of peace who died as he lived—a *Mahatma* in spirit.

Francois Marie Arouet De Voltaire

If the pen be mightier than the sword, to the sparkling wit and gnawing sarcasm of Voltaire goes the credit of struggling to create a free spirit of the French Revolution much before its time. Often referred to as the conscience of the age of enlightenment, Voltaire strove to rip open the prejudices, the hypocrisies and the vanities of his age with his skillful penmanship. Like all libertines, his life was checkered with highs and lows. From the plethora of rich varied experience and with an eye to see what is beyond, Voltaire's writings created a sensation in Europe and earned him the nickname of "Vive Voltaire" in France.

Francois Marie Arouet De Voltaire was the youngest boy of the Notary Arouet. He was born in Paris in 1694 with a disposition so weak and unsure that hardly anyone expected the child to live. But the baby survived. It was destined to life of distinction by the clever use of his intellectual faculties. Amongst the men of letters of his time, the crown would unsurpassingly belong to none other than Voltaire.

At the age of three Voltaire could recite the whole of La Fontaine's fables. His godfather the Abbe de Chateauneuf had a great influence on the boy. The Abbe's unconventional views and his unorthodox beliefs introduced Voltaire to the world of free thought. The Mosaide an agnostic poem, Voltaire learnt early and much of his later work was written in the same strain. Voltaire's battle with orthodox religion began early and he never laid down the cudgels to rest.

Voltaire attended the Jesuit school where he excelled. His intelligence and quick wit won him admiration and it was a severe blow to his father when Voltaire declined a profession in law. He opted instead to be a man of letters. His father's desire to procure him a post as a royal advocate was declined with a polite rejoinder, "I will make a position for myself that costs nothing."

Under the chartered direction of his godfather Voltaire was introduced to the halls of royalty. Here he displayed his talent by writing epigrams, lampoons and later drama. His first tragedy, Oedipus was quite a success. The year was 1715 and Louis XIV was dead. France under the reign of Louis XV was far from a free spirited society. Oedipus was peppered with scathing allusions to tyranny and bigotry. This bold criticism of the Regent's libertine lifestyle brought Voltaire behind bars. He was thrown in the Bastille for 11 months. He was released just in time for the premiere of Oedipus. It broke box office records at the Comedie Francaise. At 24, Voltaire was famous.

Next Voltaire wrote his long epic on Henri IV, entitled Henriade. The permission for the publication of the poem was not granted for it dealt with the subject of Protestantism and religious tolerance.

In the French elite Voltaire soon gained reputation of the rapier wit. Though not bestowed with physical beauty, he charmed the girls and courtly ladies alike. They hung on to every word he said. His passion for the actress Adrienne Lecouvreur, brought him face to face with a rival -the Chevalier de Rohan, scion of one of France's noblest families. The latter scoffing at the commonness of Voltaire's lineage said, "Monsieur Arouet? Monsieur Voltaire? What really is your name?" Quick to take an insult Voltaire replied, "Voltaire. I am the first of my line as you are the last of yours!" After a surprise confrontation with the Rohan's lackeys, Voltaire challenged him to a duel. A royalist could hardly fight a commoners Voltaire soon found himself midst the high walls of the Bastille once more. He was released only to be exiled to England.

England's free air opened new vistas before him and Voltaire found himself enthralled by the glitterati of the literary world. Swift, Pope, Congreve and a host of others were now acquaintances with whom he exchanged ideas and thoughts. The English toleration and respect for freedom was refreshing change for Voltaire. Ideas of Bolingbroke and other deists had a great impact on Voltaire. He dedicated an edition of Henriade to Queen Caroline and wrote The History of Charles XII. He became the first French writer to speak English fluently and first to translate Shakespeare.

On reaching Paris in 1729, Voltaire found himself once again at daggers end with the Establishment. The question was once again ethical. Adriene Lecouvreur, mortally ill but playing in a Voltaire tragedy to the last, died in the author's arms. In accordance with the church practices which looked down on the theatre, her body was secretly taken to a common burial place. This incensed Voltaire, whose recent visit to England had made him aware of the honour the actors and actress deserved and must receive. He penned an Ode to his dishonoured mistress and then wrote the English Letters which praised Britain over France in all spheres. The Letters were a direct insult to the French society and in 1734 the work was burnt by a public executioner and a warrant issued for Voltaire's arrest. Voltaire eluding the police found refuge in an admirer Emilie Masquise du Chatelet at her chateau in Champagne. The Marquise though eleven years his junior and married without children, shared a great love of the theater with Voltaire. She also an avid student of astronomy, chemistry and philosophy. She helped to develop Voltaire's interest in these subjects. There grew to be a mutual relationship based on love and friendship between the two. But the lovers broke up when Madame du Chatelet's attention was taken up by the more charming Saint Lambert. She soon died after giving birth to a little girl and Voltaire was beside himself with grief.

At this time he was invited by King Frederick of Prussia. Voltaire was happy there for a while until his blunt and brazen tongue got him once again into trouble. His merciless criticism of the unscrupulous, avaricious tyranny of the King made him an unwelcome guest. Voltaire in disgust described his task of correcting Frederick's poems as "washing the King's dirty linen."

Voltaire soon found himself without a place or a patron. His return to Paris was unimaginable because his liaison with King Frederick of Prussia, automatically made him a member of the enemy camp in Paris. Voltaire brought the estate of Ferney, near the Swiss frontier. It enabled him to skip across to his residence of Le Delices (now a Voltaire museum), near Geneva when his controversial pen aroused anger of the French authorities.

At Ferney his practical creativity found an outlet. He created a model and farms. He developed scientific methods of reforestation, imported silkworms and started a watch factory. It was a mini utopia where Protestants and Catholics lived in harmony. Voltaire's business acumen made him find clients for his watches in Catherine of Russia and Sultan of Turkey. He devoted his vitriolic pen to particular causes. Through concrete effort he was able to vindicate Jean Calas after his frightful torture and execution for the alleged murder of his son. He prevented the Chevalier de la Barre from being burned alive. Voltaire in all his sincerity stove to mitigate the harsh criminal laws.

The years at Ferney were the most productive for Voltaire. At Ferney he wrote Candide, the work that ranked him as a genius of irony and mature introspection. The work stands unsurpassed even today among the classics of world literature. This success opened the portals of happiness for Voltaire once again. He regained the lost friendship of Frederick and France once again opened her arms to welcome him.

At the age of eighty three, on completing the tragedy Irene, he returned to his beloved Paris to view the performance. At the Comedie Francaise the gala performance of Irene, the theater thundered and roared with applause and "Vive Voltaire" resonated through the walls. An actor placed a laurel wreath on the wizened head and the playwright with tears streaming down his face said, "Do you wish me to die of glory?" The captivated audience looked on and paused as they witnessed on of the most precious moments in literary history.

Two months after the triunphnal coronations, wreaths and laurals, on May 30, 1778, Voltaire passed away midst friends and admirers who viewed for a last glance of this legendary mind. It was in Voltaire's valuable work that France first heard the notes of liberty, equality and fraternity. France recognized its indebtedness and paid a great tribute to him with the inscription on the tomb that read: "He taught us how to become free."

Benjamin Franklin

For the Americans, Franklin was always 'Old dependable, intelligent and praise worthy. He was to them their very own emissary representing America in all that it stood for. The many mantles that Benjamin Franklin wore are hard to define. A man with a scientific genius, a canny businessman, a revolutionary, a philosopher and a wit - Benjamin Franklin was all this and much more.

Franklin was born in humble origins in Boston USA, in 1706, the fifteenth of the seventeen children of a poor candlemaker. At the age of 12 he was apprenticed to his half-brotherJames, a printer. At Philadelphia he gained experience with various printers and finally he opened his own printing shop. The business of printing was a mere stepping stone to success. He ventured into writing and then to publishing that put him on the road to fame. Franklin's enterprenurship was one factor that spurred him on and made him a household name across the globe.

Franklin's tryst with writing began in his teens and the attraction never ebbed thereafter. He began writing unsigned or pseudonymous ballads and satires. He would slip these under his brother's door, who would publish them unsuspectingly. Franklin's linguistic abilities made him a master of many languages. Latin, French, German. Italian, Spanish were languages he spoke with flaire. Being a voracious reader he devoured books on science and philosophy. His autobiography and books on home spun maxims have made delightful reading material for generations to come. Over the years his publications grew and at the age of twenty six he initiated the Poor Richard's Almanack.

As a politician he fought for colonies in London before the Revolution. He published a satiric piece that lashed out at Britain's imperialism entitled - Rules by which a great empire may be reduced to a small one. With vigorous energy his satire spelled out the "rules" i. e. the injustices suffered by colonies. His secular humanitarian approach made him an endearing figure in the international political scenario.

Franklin's dedication to his country was exemplary. Even when a prosperous businessman of the publishing world, his allegiance to his country never took a back seat. An active participant in the American Revolution he even took up many civic projects in the ensuing years. He set in motion the first professional police force and the first volunteer fire company in Philadelphia, the first American fire-insurance company, the University of Pennsylvania and the world famous Pennsylvania Hospital.

Franklin's intellect and broadminded approach to things made him a key figure in American politics. He was the first statesman to build on the concept of a united nation. He invented the American dual system of state government united under a federal authority, two decades before the Revolutionary War.

Ingeniously he solved the political problems that arose in the aftermath of the War of Independence. His sagacious handling of the near collapse of the constitutional convention in Philadelphia won him respect that few can equal. The small states wanted equal representation in the Congress and the big ones wanted delegations based on population. Franklin engineered the compromise under which the senate is based on the first plan and the House of Representatives on the second.

Franklin's achievement in the field of science has placed him amongst the pioneers of scientists on whose achievements we today stand successful. Apart from drawing electricity from a cloud on a kite string, he created the first viable theory of electicity. He dispelled the theory that lightning and electricity were two separate forces. Franklin proved that they are the same thing. The terms "positive" and "negative" were introduced to us by Franklin. The concepts of battery, conductor, electrical charge and discharge were defined by Franklin. He invented the electrical condenser, used today in every radio, television and telephone circuit. To him goes the credit of inventing the lighting rod, that removed forever the terror from people's lives. His studies always promoted practical results. He invented the chemical fertilizer, the Franklin stove and bifocal spectacles. While chartering the Gulf Stream he discovered that storms rotate while traveling forward and that this explained the watersprouts at sea.

Franklin's humour often had a scientific base. On a windy day in England he noticed waves on the surface of a brook. He told a group of friends that he could 'magically' calm the waters. Slipping upstream alone, he poured some oil from the unscrewed top of his cane into the water. Slowly the waves subsided and all that his friends could do was to give him a hearty applause. This aura of mystery never left him and won him quite a reputation.

Nothing elucidates Franklin's life better than his own maximum, "God helps them that help themselves. "His life was a story of constant endeavour and the desire to achieve. His pragmatic insight that social institutions are made not by Divine Will but by men made him an instant hero in France in 1770. He was to the French that divine spark of liberty that questioned the rule of tyranny that had infested the social structures of France for generations. He was the liberator who "snatched the lightning from the skies and the scepters from the tyrants."

To the royal structures of Britain, he was in contrast a dangerous man, sprung from the new libertine culture of America. A dangerous man, he held the deadly weapon that unleashed chaotic liberty. The stiff upper lipped annals of power and royalty, crumbled under his scatting satire. His revolutionary spirit celebrated the song of liberty and individual freedom.

In 1770 Franklin died. the French National Assembly went into mourning for three days. Biographer Car Van Doren summed up his life saying, "Mind and will, talent and art, strength and ease, wit and grace met in him as if nature had been lavish and happy when he was shaped." But perhaps the best tribute came from Comte de Mirabeau, the great French Revolutionary orator who called Franklin the philosopher who did most to extend the rights of man over the earth, "Antiquity would have raised altars to this mighty genius."

Amelia Earheart

The early 1920's were yet to witness the wave of feminism and the society even in the west was essentially male dominated. It was at such a time in a New York office in the year 1928 that George Palmer Putman, publisher, author, enterpreneur was sitting at his desk and waiting. He was looking for a female candidate pilot to take up a vacancy on the plane Friendship, that was to make a transatlantic flight. The candidate had to be a young willing woman willing to risk her life, at no pay simply for the sake of adventure. It seemed in the day an arduous task to find a woman who was both modest and dignified and was ready to face death with composure if the time so arrived. Putman's prayers were answered in the person of Amelia Earhart. Freckled, graceful with a pair of slate-gray eyes, Amelia fulfilled all the credentials required by Putman. She was a social service worker with a passion for flying. She became the first woman to fly over the formidable waters of the Atlantic.

Amelia Earhart was born in 1898, the daughter of a Kansas lawyer. Like the other children of the U. S. Middle West, Amelia's life followed a set pattern. But unlike other girls her age, she showed a passion more for improvising break-neck slides from hayloft to the floor of her grandfather's barn than playing with dolls. Fishing, riding astride and gymnastics were the fields that she pursued with enthusiasm. In school she was termed as the "girl in brown who walks alone. "She even pioneered in the wearing of the first pair of bloomers ever to glaze the eyes of Atchison, Kansass. After leaving secondary school during the last year of the First World War she served as a nurse's help.

Armistice set her thinking about her future. She tried to look for a job that would satisfy her urge to do something unconventional. She tried her hand at photography, motor-car repairing and she even spent one year in pre-medical work. Then, in 1920, Edwin Earhart took his daughter to her first air meet, in California. Amelia discovered her destiny.

The fascination of seeing a plane was novel. Amelia was sepellbound. She hopped in the aircraft for a "joy ride" only to discover that the cascading ground hundreds of feet beneath her and the dizzying heights to which she had climbed made her adreline flow in full force and strengthened her decision to reach for the skies. The haunting cadence of the skies echoed her resolve to sing the music of the heavens forever. It was quite a surprise to Frank Hawks and a fellow pilot that this young lady did not get into hysterics.

Amelia received the Federation Aeronautique International license in 1923. She was the first woman to soar to fourteen thousand feet, and one of the first American fliers to experiment with air-cooled engines. Even with this astounding feet to her credit Amelia could not make the aeronautics industry treat her seriously. In 1926, Amelia settled down to social service in Boston as flying as a hobby was too expensive to persue. Two years later while she was attending to a group of Chinese and Syrian toddlers Amelia received a phone call that made all her dreams come true. The phone call was from George Putman and he was inviting her to join a crew of three members in a transatlantic flight. The plane was a tri-motor Fokker, equipped with floats and the pilot was none other than the famous Wilmer Stulzt and his mechanic "Slim" Gordon. As Amelia's heart beat faster she heard herself saying, "Yes, I'd be willing."

In June17, 1928 on her flight aboard the Friendship Amelia spurred interest all over America. Millions stayed close to their radios that memorable Sunday. Everyone wanted to know who the brave, reckless girl was and all so thoroughly misguided. Friendship with Amelia on board, crawled its way out of the Trepassey Harbour in New found land and pressed its nose eastward against the clotting fog.

The voyage was more than twenty four hours long. Eighteen hours of the time was spent in challenging conditions. The pilot flew through blinding storms, through solid poultices of fog. The plane dropped to shake ice from its ledges and sometimes it climbed to escape the waves. To combat hungry headwinds the plane consumed fuel and the motor strained under the overload. The radio drew a blank. Midst icy cascades and only sixty minutes of fuel in the tank Amelia wrote her impressions of the flight. It might as well have been her last flight. Her jotting were those of a dreamer and a practical piolt. They were later published in a book that became an instant bestseller. Poetry mingled with gay drawings and observations that revealed clouds as "fantastic gobs of mashed potatoes appealed to the public. They could identify with the writer who was it seemed to them just like them.

The Friendship landed at Burry Port, Whales, the eleventh heavier-than -air machine to complete the North Atlantic crossing. Amelia's Earhart's luggage for the journey was a comb and a toothbrush.

The Aeronautics industry embraced her. Amelia had become a celebrity the world over. For the next four years she became the super saleswoman of an expanding industry. Proffessional aviation opened its doors to her, and she slogged out distance records, pioneered the auto-gyro, tested experimental planes and engines, gave instruction, boosted air travel with articles and lectures. Amelia became a rage in West and emerged as the new woman of the day who spoke a language that crossed the sexist barriers. Men admired her femininity and women were charmed by her modesty and her sincere championing of their daughter's careers in the field. George Putman married her.

The spirit of adventure kept her going. She experimented with celestial navigation, radio communication and dead reckoning. She let herself be blindfold in innumerable cockpits and tried instrumental flying. After she had to her credit more than a thousand hours of flying she finally decided that she was ready for what seemed to be her heart's closest desire - a transatlantic solo. Only Lindbergh had accomplished that.

On May 20 1932, Amelia climbed into the cockpit of her single-engine Lockheed-Vega at Harbour Grace, Newfoundland. Fourteen hours and fifty-six minutes later in a pasture at Londonderry, Ireland an alarming red machine belching blue smoke and flames landed among the grazing cows. Amelia had set a new world record under unfavourable conditions. With a broken altimeter and a flaming manifold ring Amelia had decided to carry on regardless. For five hours she flew by instruments through pummeling storms. The tachometer failed and there was a leaking fuel gauge not four feet from the blazing manifold ring. The result was that the plane was filled with fumes and Amelia was forced to make that decision to step down at the very first opportunity.

Amelia's transatlantic solo secured her a permanent place in the aviation archives. Her spirit of adventure inspired many and she became the woman of her day. Her flashing smile and her warm personality made her an endearing figure across the globe. With the laurels of fame and recognition at her beckoning Amelia Earhart remained a simple girl. Her head remained unturned.

On her flight from Honolulu to California in 1935, Amelia sat snug in her cabin near the microphone giving vent to her poetic soul. She said "The moon set and I was alone with the stars. I have often said that the lure of flying is the lure of beauty, and I need no other flight to convince me . . . . "Ten thousand people were waiting at Oakland Airport to meet her. But the plane never landed. Destiny in an ironic way fulfilled Amelia's prognosis. She had said, "Some day I'll get bumped off. I don't want to go, but when I go I'd like to go in my plane . Quickly. "A flight around the world was her final challenge with nature. She had said before the flight, "I mean to give up long-distance flights. I have a feeling that there is just about one more good flight left in my system and I hope this is it. "

With navigator Fred Noonan Amelia took off in the new twin engined Lockheed Electra. They went from Honolulu to distant Howland Island, north of Samoa. They first went to Lae New Guinea. They had twenty two thousand nine hundred miles behind them. Ahead, more than two thousand five hundred miles across the loneliest water in the world lay Howland. On July 2, 1937, Amelia and Noonan took off. The last contact that the plane had was with a Coastguard cutter who picked up a message in a familiar voice. "Headwinds. . . half an hour's gas. . . circling. "The plane was lost not a hundred miles from Howland . Amelia's luck ran out.

Amelia Earhart's spirit soared for individualism that sought to free itself from the binding conventions of society . It strove to liberate the self in doing what it believed in most dearly. Brave, noble and dignified the spirit of Amelia Earhart lives on in every individual's desire to reach for the skies.

Charles Darwin

To posterity the name of Charles Darwin is familiar. He is the naturalist whose theories rocked the basic assumptions of a God created universe and put forward a theory based on Natural Selection and the survival of the fittest. His findings decentralized the warmth of the hearth wherein all was according to God's plan. His theory of evolution made the basis of our existence scientific and rendered theology obsolete.

It was His Britannic Majesty's brig Beagle that Darwin's theories first began to take shape. In 1831 on a surveying expedition around the world Darwin was the ship's naturalist. Only twenty two and fresh from Cambridge Darwin was of a sensitive and a shy disposition. This was peppered by an inquisitive mind that sought answers and explanations to all that it was confronted with. Darwin refused to take anything on face value. His unflaggingly curious mind sought an explanation to everything.

On their exploration one of the first stops was on the uninhabited Galapagos Islands, hundreds of miles off the coast of South America, in the loneliest doldrums of the Pacific. The place was a naturalist's delight. Darwin was confronted with a variety of species from the animal kingdom that challenged as the mysteries of their existence prodded his keen mind. It presented a living museum of the past geological times, where giant lizards which ought to have been extinct long ago mingled with huge land tortoises. Enormous crabs and gaudy sea lions infested the area. In this virgin garden of Eden so unaccustomed were the animals to the presence of man that a hawk allowed itself to be knocked off a tree with a stick and ground doves settled trustingly on the explorers' shoulders. Darwin's delight at this unexplored natural habitat stretched before him knew no bounds. The islands presented a fertile ground for study and Dawin discovered that though the islands seemingly similar in soil and climate had their own peculiar fauna. Ecah island presented a species ostensibly similar but on closer look all of them differed. None of the islands had quite the same species.

Darwin's close observations made him record that though the islands were close together each had a different species of finches, ground doves, lizards, tortoises, insects and snails. This arbitrary creation of different species foxed Darwin. In one of his first recordings he wrote, "One might fancy, that one species had been modified for different ends. On these small, barren, rocky islands we seem to be brought nearer to the mystery of mysteries, the first appearance of new beings on earth." In a daringly subtle way Darwin had started to question the authority of the Genesis and also the belief of the scientists of the time.

Darwin's fascinating findings continued for the five years that he on board the ship. They sailed to Tahiti, New Zealand, Tasmania, Australia, Ascension Island, the Cape Verdes, and the Azores. Throughout the voyage Darwin was haunted by the single observation of closely related but differing species. He was on the brink of exploding the complacent explanation of a God centered universe. But it was a while before he made his theories public.

By way of fascinating letters and splendid collection Darwin was quite a name when he finally arrived in Enland. He won praise and acclaim for his work on the origin of atolls and his studies on marine life. But his observations and findings of the voyage were not made public and were recorded in a little pocket not-book wherein he set down all the evidence he could gather to support his theory of evolution. Darwin visited plant and animal breeders and studied their records in minute details. He bought pigeons and raising them studied them closely. He found that the domestic pigeons all descended from the common blue rock dove. He also observed that pouters, fan-tails, carriers and tumblers so differed from one another, as a result of centuries of selection by fanciers, that a zoologist would if he came on them in the wild, classify them as separate varieties. Be it animals or stains of wheat the same process was in motion. Darwin realized that evolution did not belong to a long forgotten past but was going on right before our eyes.

After working for twenty years on his theory Darwin at last confided to a friend, "At last, gleams of light have come, and I am almost convinced (quite contrary to the opinion that I started with) that species are not (it is like confessing a murder) immutable. "At this point he had little thought of publishing his findings of two hundred and thirty one pages. It was only on confronting the theory of Alfred Russel of the East Indies that Dawin decided to make his work public. He met Russel and exchanged the similarity of their findings. Russel had also come to evolve the theory of evolution by way of natural selection. He wrote, "There is no limit of variability to a species, as formerly supposed. The life of wild animals is a struggle for existence. The abundance or rarity of a species depends upon its more or less perfect adaptation to the conditions of existence. Useful variations will tend to increase, useless or hurtful variations to diminish. Superior varieties will ultimately expatriate the original species. There is a tendency in Nature to progression by minute steps." Darwin and Russel decided to go into publication jointly and presented a new theory of evolution by natural selection at the next meeting of the learned Linnaean Society.

The theory of evolution stated that continuing from generation to generation, natural selection tends to pile up enough small differences to amount to a major difference and that is evolution. The Linnaean society listened patiently but did not give their acceptance to the theories presented by the two. If accepted the theory would make redundant the life work of so many older men. On the other hand, the hitherto mysterious fossils of extinct animals and plants began to offer a picture of continuing creation more astounding than the literal Biblical explanation. The discoveries never reached the public ear but were locked away in the unreachable portals of scientific thought.

The following year Darwin published The Origin of Species and brought upon himself the heat of controversy. He was hailed as a genius and as a mad man at the same time. He was the creator of scientific anarchy and his was the blasphemy that had soiled the sanctity of the church. Darwin's book though brought out with great apprehension by the publisher sold out the very first day of the publication. It was an instant best seller and Darwin was an international name.

The book opened the floodgates of controversy and the church seethed with anger. The book was declared totally amoral and the fundamentalist Victorians spoke sharply against the contents. Bishop Samuel Wilberforce accepted a challenge of a debate at Oxford against Darwin's fiery young champion, the biologist Thomas Huxley. "Soapy Sam" as the Bishop was nicknamed by the rationales had little training in science and depended more on ridicule to get his point across. Midst the debate addressing his opponent he sneered, "Does the gentleman, claim to be descended from a monkey on his mother's side or his father's?" Springing to his feet the young Huxley retorted, "I would far rather be descended from a monkey on both my parents' sides than from a man who uses his brilliant talents for arousing religious prejudice in discussions of subjects about which he knows nothing." The well phrased retort got the irreverent Oxford students exited and the final applause was for Huxley and therefore Darwin's.

As for Darwin he spent his days in the country. His health after the voyage on the Beagle was always precarious. He tried to retain tranquillity in his home at Kent. His work in the laboratory kept him occupied and The Descent of Man, The Expression of Emotions in Men and Animals were writing that stirred the world and put him in the center of fresh controversy. But Darwin carried on regardless. His uncontroversial work on the study of orchids and their fertilization and the methods by which primroses prevent inbreeding managed to quell the rage that his other more volatile work raked.

The work of later scientists have managed to further strengthen Darwin's theory of evolution. Mendel's work on inheritance and Genetics as a science was unborn in Darwin's day and nor had De Vries worked out his mutation theory. All these later findings have tried to complete the theory of evolution first propounded by Darwin. He was the first to unshakably state the facts of evolution. The term evolution came into being with Darwin and has lived on for centuries. Constant change that is the cycle of life and this great secret was unveiled by Darwin.

This gentle old fellow grown grey in the quest of knowledge was always a silent humble figure with a belief in his findings but never boisterously shouting for support. Infact it was hard to believe that this humble man was the center of controversy that had questioned the very foundation of thought in his times. At the rare scientific meetings that he attended the entire audience would rise and cheer this dear old man whose unmitigated attention to the cause of science never flagged.

On April 19, 1882, Charles Darwin died. Thus ended his intellectual adventure. He was buried in Westminister Abbey by pall bearers who included Huxley, Wallace and James Russel Lowell. He was laid to rest beside the body of Sir Issac Newton. So rests the finest type of Homo Sapiens that ever touched the life of man. His zealous search for knowledge and his utter delight in children and flowers were the only passions that marked his life. Though a scientist with a questing spirit never by word of his was God denied, nor the soul of man.

Louis Braille

The credit of providing sight to the sightless in the dark goes to a Frenchman called Louis Braille. He invented the Braille system of reading for the blind and opened a whole new world of knowledge for the blind to explore. Braille's system became so much a part of education for the blind that as far back as 1895 the inventor's very name was spelt as a common noun. Today even the Chinese use the system. A number of magazines are published every month in Braille. But Braille's own initiation in the work for the blind stems from a story that is heartrending in itself.

A son of a saddle maker, Louis Braille was a little boy with sparkling eyes. Often, he would play besides his working father. In the year 1812, tragedy struck . One day playfully clutching two sharp awls, Louis ran out of the shop. He stumbled and fell. Louis lost one eye in the accident and soon became totally blind.

Dependent now on the cane Louis's life no doubt must have been one of severe dejection and frustrations. The villagers of the little village were by the number of tappings of his cane know where he was headed to. This method of tapping was ingeniously implemented by Braille in the system of reading for the blind that he was to invent later on. This system was called by Braille the system of "frozen taps."

Louis attended the Institution Nationale des Jeunes Aveugles, a school for the blind in Paris at the age of ten. Here Louis was taught the alphabet by Valentine Hauy. Hauy patiently guided Louis' fingers along the twenty six letters of the alphabet that were made from twigs. From these Louis soon learnt to read books that were made up of letters cut out of cloth and pasted on pages. Each letter was three inches in height and two inches wide. A fable narrated in this fashion would on an average take up seven thick books each weighing about eight pounds. Soon the book was improvised and embossed letters helped the pupils to read. But this too was a daunting task for the letters had to be atleast an inch high for the pupils to get a proper feel. Louis, so eager to learn had to wait patiently to read all that his heart desired.

Louis' desire was to unleash the world of books to the blind who were so utterly lonely. He spent a lot of his time trying to devise a code with symbols for words and phrases. He tried codes based on triangles, squares and circles, each bearing variations representing different letters, but none of them worked out.

Louis soon took up a post of a teacher at the Institution Nationale des Jeunes Aveugles. One day sitting in a cafe listening to the news being read out by his friend he heard about an army officer who had developed a system of writing in raised dots and dashes, to be used in the darkness. The message could be read by touch without the need for striking light. Louis exited at this new breakthrough that could perhaps, open a whole new world of experince. Braille thrilled said, ". . . I have solved the impenetrable problem of the blind-broken their age long death like trance."

Braille worked out the concepts of the system that was to lighten the dark recesses of the mind of the blind with the light of the written word. With an awl the impressions were punched into the thick black paper so that small protuberances could be felt on the other side. A simple army code had been set up:one dot might mean "advance", two dots "retreat", and so on.

Braille decided to try and build a code for the entire language. Enthralled with the new possibilities that the new system had opened Braille said to the Captain, "Let me be the world's first blind to thank you."

For five years Braille worked tirelessly trying to perfect the system by which the blind could read. It was ironical that the same instrument that had blinded him was responsible in developing the system. Using a key of six holes in an oblong, Braille developed sixty three possible combinations which besides the alphabet, supplied symbols for punctuation, contractions and short words like "and" and "for."

Braille paid homage to the great blind poet John Milton when he prepared sections of the poet's work in his system. He said, "It is fitting that I draw upon the sightless poet for the first adaptation." But strangely enough Braille had to face a lot of hurdles before his system finally received acceptance. Although he could "punch-write" almost as fast as anyone could dictate to him he was labeled as a cheat by jealous colleagues. They accused him of memorizing the passages he chose to demonstrate. Braille appealed to the French Academy to accept this system but he was turned down ungraciously for the authorities felt that the blind received adequate training under the prevailing embossing system. But Braille received support from the students whom he trained secretly to use the system. Apart from the language he taught them to punch out mathematical symbols and solve equations. He also worked out a Braille musical code and became a skilled organist.

Braille's health had been frail throughout his life. It was not until his last illness that his system gained acceptane. A student of his giving a piano recital tapped her way to the lip of the stage. On receiving a hearty applause, addressing the audience she said, "... Your applause is not for me. It belongs to a man who is dying ..." She then told the public about the educative and useful Braille method that had introduced a blind girl like her to the magic of music. She narrated how it was the jealousies of the older colleagues that had kept the system closeted and was thereby denying horizon to millions of deaf all over the world. The crowd charged with emotion demanded acceptance of the Braille's system and the news made headlines.

Louis Braille was on his deathbed when the news of his success came to him. He was beside himself with joy and through tears streaming down his face he said, "This is the third time in my life I have permitted myself to weep. First when I was blinded. Second, when I heard about the 'night writing., And now because I know that my life is not a failure."

On his death a bust of Braille's was erected outside the saddler's shop at Coupvray. The bust is endowed with the most compassionate eyes. A tribute by the artist to the man who lit up many a darkened soul. But, perhaps the best tribute came from his pupil who said, "He has not only given the blind of the world windows, but he has given them music to weep by."

Wolfgang Amadeus Mozart

The long and winding streets of Salzburg have an undoubtedly romantic association with the maestro and legendary composer Wolfgang Amadeus Mozart. Echoing with his music, many of amateur musician today cannot help but aspire to achieve magic of Mozart's compositions. Getting even a strain of that soulful music that the spontaneous magical fingers of Mozart is a joyous achievement.

Born January 27, 1756, in Salzburg, and baptized Johannes Chrysostomus Wolfgangus Theophilus Mozart, he was educated by his father, Leopold Mozart, who was concertmaster in the court orchestra of the archbishop of Salzburg and a celebrated violinist, composer, and author.

When Leopald gave music lessons to Wolfgang's sister, Maria Anna, "Nannerl," the little boy watched carefully and made trials sound on the harpsichord. Seeing such mighty talent in the little boy, Leopald decided to dedicate his life to the development of the child's genius.

In 1762, both Mozart and his sister were taken to Vienna, the glittering hub of the Austrian empire and they played at the Imperial court of Francis I.

Mozart's accomplishment on the clavier, violin, and organ and was highly skilled in sight-reading and improvisation. he won the hearts of all Vienna. Five short piano pieces composed by Mozart when he was six years old are still frequently played. During his tour of Europe Wolfgang composed sonatas for the harpsichord and violin (1763), a symphony (1764), an oratorio (1766), and the opera buffa La finta semplice (The Simple Pretense, 1768). He was the most celebrated child in all of Europe. The London Public Advertiser proclaimed him, "The greatest prodigy that Europe, or even human nature, has to boast of, is without contradiction, the little German boy, Wolfgang Mozart."

Fame and success did not dampen Mozart's childish was full of mischief and it was difficult to believe that such music of the spirit was born of the little 'elf' who like any other child was full of play and passion. His hazel eyes shone with excitement as he, "ran about the room with a stick between his legs by way of a horse."

In 1769 Mozart was appointed concertmaster to the archbishop of Salzburg, and later in the same year, at La Scala (Milan, Italy), he was made a chevalier of the Order of the Golden Spur by the pope. He also composed his first German operetta, Bastien und Bastienne, in the same year. At the age of 14 he was commissioned to write a serious opera. This work, Mitridate, rè di Ponto (Mithridates, King of Pontus, 1770), produced under his direction at Milan, completely established an already phenomenal reputation. The performance was repeated 20 times before full houses.

The Mozarts returned to Salzburg in 1771. Hieronymus, count von Colloredo, the successor to the archbishop of Salzburg, who had died while the Mozarts were touring Italy, cared little for music. Mozart's appointment at Salzburg, however, proved to be largely honorary; it allowed ample time for a prodigious musical output during his next six years, but afforded little financial security.

Disappointed Mozart headed for Mannheim with the thought of making a career in music at the royal court. Here he received accolade but not a job. He continued to work for the Archbishop Hieronymus Colloredo, who treated him not much better than a servant. Mozart had to eat his meals with the other servants, valets and cooks. But the love and the passion of music and a basic means of a livelihood kept him going. It was only when Colleredo forbade him from giving concerts on his own in Vienna, that Mozart left. He went to Vienna where his heart was.

, Mozart met the Weber family once again. He had met them earlier at Mannheim, where he had fallen in love with one of their daughters. That daughter now was married to an actor but the younger one, Constanze was still around. Mozart married her after a short courship. Mozart remained a devoted husband through the nine years of their marriage that ended with his death.

Vienna "a marvelous city" in Mozart's words was an ideal city for his craft and "the best place in the world. "It welcomed Mozart's genius with open arms and Mozart achieved the status of a celebrity with all of Vienna yearning for more of that wonderful Mozartian music. Here he progressed from the traditional harpsichord to the still newfangled piano, with its sweeter sound. He composed operas that placed him in an unchallenged position amongst the musicians of his day. In 1782 the performance of The Abduction from the Harem established his reputation. "Opera," he confessed, "is my joy and passion." It was his adaptation of Lorenzo da Ponte of Beaumarchais'revolutionary play, The Marriage of Figro that Mozat's brilliance shone in every single note. Fiagro was received with something like a delirious joy by the audience and made Mozart a raging hit.

When Mozart and da Ponte were commissioned by Prague to compose another opera they chose to do a spine-chilling version of the old legend of Don Giovanni—the super male who having broken every moral law, gets his comeuppance in the end. Most of Mozart's music deals with the belief in the with the nobility of man and the triumph of good over evil. The Magic Flute is resonant of the Freemasons - an idealistic brotherhood that was attracting many of the generation. It was premiered on September 30, 1791, merely five weeks before Mozart's death.

While Mozart was working on the singspiel The Magic Flute (1791), an emissary of a Count Walsegg mysteriously requested a requiem mass. Wolfgang began to work on it by fits and starts, composing passages of great beauty. "I'm writing my own requiem," he said to Constanze. Partial paralysis forced him to leave the work uncompleted. Dr Carl Bar, a Swiss physician, concludes that wolfgang's childhood travels, "must have left the delicate boy with the makings of illness to which he must have succumed." He died, presumably of typhoid fever, in Vienna on December 5, 1791; his burial was attended by few friends. The place of his grave is unmarked. The legend that the Italian composer Antonio Salieri murdered him is unsupported by reputable scholars.

Mozart's last few years were bereft of the idolatry fame that had swept him on in entrance into Vienna. The joyous outbursts of "Bravo Mozart!" did not last and the Viennese people began to look for new talent. This dejection and his failing health may have been two reasons for his premature end.

Mozart's creative method was extraordinary, for his manuscripts show that, although he made an occasional preliminary sketch of a difficult passage, he almost invariably thought out a complete work before committing it to paper. His music combines classical style of the 18th century, the goal of which was to be succinct, clear, and well balanced while at the same time developing ideas to a point of emotionally satisfying fullness. These qualities are perhaps best expressed in his concerts, with their dramatic contrasts between a solo instrument and the orchestra, and in his operas, with their profound contrasts between different personalities reacting to changing situations. His operas achieved a new unity of vocal and instrumental writing; they are marked by subtle characterization and an unusual use of classic symphonic style in large-scale ensembles.

In his brief life-1756-1791, Mozart composed a staggering 626 compositions. These include songs, dances and sonatas, church music and concerts, some 50 symphonies and 19 operas. Most of his melodies have a haunting optimism that enthuse even a dull moment an Italian taste for clear and graceful melody with a German taste for formal and contrapuntal ingenuity. Mozart thus epitomizes the today—so many generations down the line.

Alfred Nobel

The name of Alfred Nobel is synonymous with the prizes that people receive the world over for excelling in a field. It is a rare honour to receive the prize and aspirants all over the world work hard to achieve this distinction. Nobel Prizes, awards are granted annually to persons or institutions for outstanding contributions during the previous year in the fields of physics, chemistry, physiology or medicine, literature, international peace, and economic sciences. The yearly prizes are awarded from the interest accruing from a trust fund provided by the testament of the Swedish chemist, inventor, and philanthropist Alfred Bernhard Nobel.

Today many as indebted to the generosity of this man who has not failed to serve in death the progress of humanity. According to the will of this generous, "The whole of my remaining realizable estate shall be dealt with in the following way: the capital, invested in safe securities by my executors, shall constitute a fund, the interest on which shall be annually distributed in the form of prizes to those who, during the preceding year, shall have conferred the greatest benefit on mankind. The said interest shall be divided into five equal parts, which shall be apportioned as follows: one part to the person who shall have made the most important discovery or invention within the field of physics; one part to the person who shall have made the most important chemical discovery or improvement; one part to the person who shall have made the most important discovery within the domain of physiology or medicine; one part to the person who shall have produced in the field of literature the most outstanding work of an idealistic tendency; and one part to the person who shall have done the most or the best work for fraternity between nations, for the abolition or reduction of standing armies and for the holding and promotion of peace congresses. The prizes for physics and chemistry shall be awarded by the Swedish Academy of Sciences; that for physiological or medical works by the Karolinska Institute in Stockholm; that for literature by the Academy in Stockholm, and that for champions of peace by a committee of five persons to be elected by the Norwegian Storting. It is my express wish that in awarding the prizes no consideration whatever shall be given to the nationality of the candidates, but that the most worthy shall receive the prize, whether he be a Scandinavian or not."

The story of Alfred Nobel's venture into the world of scientific invention began one day in 1891 when a group of bankers gave an important audience to a young Swede who claimed to have an oil that would blow up the globe. The Swede was not entertained and was unceremoniously turned out. But on hearing about the young Swede Napoleon III invited Alfred for a talk. Alfred returned with a draft of a hundred thousand francs. Thus the foundation of the Nobel Fortune was laid.

Alfred was the third of the four sons. His health was always delicate and his mother fought a constant battle to keep him alive. Most part of his education was done at St. Petersburg Russia . He went to the United States to study mechanical engineering. As a young man he travelled to Europe. Here he fell in love with a girl who died soon after, Heartbroken and dejected he returned to his father's factory and dedicated his life to the development of the most powerful explosives.

Alfred's father Emmanuel Nobel had been tinkering with explosives for a number of years. He was convinced that nitroglycerin had great possibilities as an explosive. In those days it was chiefly used as a stimulant in heart ailments. Alfred and his father observed the erratic behaviour of the nitroglycerine. They noticed that sometimes a small jolt could cause it to explode, while at other times a major thud would cause no sensation whatsoever. What were the conditions under which these explosives would explode? These were nagging questions and both the son and the father set out to find the answers together.

Alfred soon learnt that the only sure way of exploding this soup like liquid was to confine it in a stout container and set it off with a primary explosion. From this he evolved the blasting cap - an invention still the basis of the whole nitoglycerine. Though this was a breakthrough, taming the nitroglycerin was a long way off.

With the financial help of Lord Napoleon Alfred and his father once again set out to win the battle against the mysterious nitoglycerine. In May 1864, tragedy struck the family as the youngest son of the family, Emil Nobel, along with four other workmen were killed. Old Emmanuel was prostrated and he never did recover from the shock.

Soon the Nobel's lost the permit to work with explosives and hard times were ahead for the family. The factory cracked down. But Alfred undeterred carried on trying to experiment with the solution. He was determined to show the world that his blasting oil was safe and that it could be tamed. He moved his plant to a barge moored in a lake. He took on the responsibilities of a chemist, manufacturer, book-keeper and demonstrator all in one. So involved was he in his work that he took hardly any time to eat and in the bargain ruined his digestive system for life.

Though Alfred's aim was to use the "soup" only for peaceful purposes . Within a year the Swedish government was using his "soup" to blast a terminal railway tunnel under Stockholm, and he launched manufacturing companies in four countries.

Alfred's success at the peaceful handling of the dynamite was shortlived. Nitrogylcerine's reign of terror was about to begin. One morning in 1865, Nobel's plant in Norway soared skywards. A few weeks later, a worker in Silesia tried to cut the frozen blasting oil with an axe. They found his legs half a mile away. The following April seventy cases of nitroglycerine blew up aboard a ship docked in Panama. Even the wharf and the warehouse nearby were wrecked and another ship badly disabled. A few days later, fifteen persons were killed and a block of buildings in San Francisco by a nitoglycerine explosion in an express wagon. The world opinion turned against Alfred Nobel and on his subsequent business trip to New York he was avoided as one would the plague.

Alfred at the time had brought boxes containing the "soup". He decided to give a demonstration at a quarry and only about twenty people turned up. He wanted to educate the people that if handled properly the "soup" would behave. He poured a little of the terrible oil on a flat piece of iron, and then raised a hammer. The spectators ducked for cover. There was a sharp report but no one was harmed. Nobel in a dry scientific way he explained that only the oil struck by the hammer exploded. One couldn't blow off the lot without confining it. Then he touched a match to the puddle of oil. It burnt but it did not explode. For two hours Alfred tried to drive home the point that one could make nitrogylcerine behave the way one wanted. The crowd was convinced.

Alfred Nobel's fortunes took a turn for the better and he was swamped with orders. He became a rich man. But he also had to face some hurdles as some countries passed laws forbidding the use of Nobel's "soup." They thought that a safe nitrgylcerine had to be invented that could be easily transported without risk. Alfred Nobel invented what was termed the world over a "safe nitrogylcerine." Some say he discovered it by accident.

In northern Germany there was a light, absorbent earth called kieselguhr. One day Nobel's workers ran out of sawdust and they used the earth in packing nitroglycerine cans. The story is that one of the cans leaked, and Nobel noticed that the kieselguhr drank it up like a blotting-paper. Alfred taking up the clue mixed three parts of "soup" with one part of kieselghur and his prayers were answered. His dynamite was ready for carting without any risk. The stuff could be kneaded like putty and packed in cartridges and it was safe to ship. Nobel called it dynamite. Within ten years, fifteen Nobel plants were turning out six million pounds annually of the new explosive.

By the time Nobel was forty he was a rich, lonely man. His interests stopped outside his work. He tried to recreate his lost past life but all in vain. He bought a house in Paris. He tried his hand at writing but he could never really decide which language to write in. He was proficient in six languages. In conversation too he slipped from one to another depending on the topic of discussion. He was also a voracious reader, not only of technical books but of poetry and philosophy as well. He often discussed the latest plays and novels in the letters to his friends. He tried to write two novels that abandoned halfway and but he did manage to write a play.

Alfred's earlier loss of his lady love made him a total introvert as far as women were concerned. He harboured a more or less cynical attitude towards women in general. In his loneliness he fathomed himself to be the most repulsive man whom no woman could entertain seriously.

Loneliness led Alfred to establish the peace prize. He corresponded heavily in six languages and soon began to feel the need of a secretary. He hated hiring secretaries for he hated dismissing them. In 1876, he tried once more and Bertha Kinsky, a Bohemian countess, answered his advertisment. She was an attractive woman of thirty, well educated and a good listener. Nobel's gloomy, kindly manner appealed to her. He in turn was also much impressed. But before she actually entered her duties she ran away with the young Baron von Suttner. The couple worked for the Red Cross during the Russo-Turkish war. The Baroness was appalled by what she had seen and wrote an anti-war novel. It was at this point that she turned to Nobel for help and the Nobel became a recognized leader of the peace movement. Nobel believed that his high explosives would put an end to war sooner than the peace meetings because as military weapons became more deadly, horrified nations would disband their troops.

Nobel decided to leave his fortune which was worth two million pounds to a prize for distinguished peace workers, Later he included the prizes for science and literature. He intended these awards as to work as an inspiration for sinking geniuses.

In addition to a cash award, each Nobel Prize winner also receives a gold medal and a diploma bearing the winner's name and field of achievement. The judges often have divided the prize for achievement in a particular field among two or three people. Dividing the prize among more than three people is not allowed. If more than three people are judged to be deserving of the prize, it is awarded jointly. The fund is controlled by the board of directors of the Nobel Foundation, which serves for two-year periods and consists of six members: five elected by the trustees of the awarding bodies mentioned in the will, and the sixth appointed by the Swedish government. The six members are either Swedish or Norwegian citizens. To further the purposes of the foundation, separate institutes have been established, in accordance with Nobel's will, in Sweden and Norway for advancement of each of the five original fields for which the prizes are awarded. The first Nobel Prizes were awarded on December 10, 1901.

Nobel lived his last days in the solitude of San Remo, Italy. He spent most of time working on synthetic rubber and artificial silk. His heart began to give out and he had a laugh when the doctors prescribed nitroglycerine. When his brother, who had made a fortune in oil died, the French papers thought that it was Alfred Nobel. Alfred had the peculiar satisfaction of reading his own obituries. They were not complimentary. The French Government, had earlier on put restrictions upon his work when they were told that Alfred had sold some of the smokeless powder to Italy. On 10 December, 1896, he died.

Buddha

The founder of "Buddhism" was Gautam Buddha who lived in India some five hundred years before Christ. The name is a combination of the family name 'Gautam' and 'Buddha' which means the enlightened one. Buddhism today is divided into two major branches known to their respective followers as Theravada, the Way of the Elders, and Mahayana, the Great Vehicle. Followers of Mahayana refer to Theravada using the derogatory term Hinayana, the Lesser Vehicle. Buddhism has been significant not only in India but also in Sri Lanka, Thailand, Cambodia, Myanmar (formerly known as Burma), and Laos, where Theravada has been dominant; Mahayana has had its greatest impact in China, Japan, Taiwan, Tibet, Nepal, Mongolia, Korea, and Vietnam, as well as in India. The number of

Buddhists worldwide has been estimated at between 150 and 300 million. The reasons for such a range are twofold: Throughout much of Asia religious affiliation has tended to be non-exclusive; and it is especially difficult to estimate the continuing influence of Buddhism in Communist countries such as China.

Gautam Buddha was born Kapilavastu, that is in present day Nepal. He was the son of the head of the Sakya warrior's caste and he was called Siddharth. Though living a life of luxury, Siddharth felt dissatisfied with the pointless existence of a royal life. Toeing his father's wishes he had married and was blessed with a son. He was twenty nine years old when he decided to give up the life of luxury and follow the ascetic path.

Legend has it that, one day in 533, he came upon a sick man, an old man and a corpse. He was perturbed by the sufferings of all three and realized that suffering was common to all of mankind. He then met a monk whose worldly detachment made him look calm and serene. Gautam decided to follow his path and give up his worldly existence. He walked out at midnight without a word to anybody. It was anguish to him as he stood by his sleeping wife and son. But he turned away, responding to the calling that was in him much stronger. Siddharth was on his way to look for enlightenment. This day is celebrated by Buddhists all over the world as the Great Renunciation.

Among the ascetics the fame of Buddha spread "like the sound of a great gong in the sky." He had five followers who were impressed by his gift of application of what he believed in. At first Buddha thought that a path of rigid self-mortification was the way to salvation. One day after six years of self-mortification, when he was attacked by violent pains he fell dead faint. This made him realize that in order to break open the secrets of the universe one has to adopt a "middle way," between ascetic self denial and sensual indulgence. This was considered a sacrilege in those days and Gautam was abandoned by his five followers and he had to search for wisdom all alone.

Gautam's way of thought was akin to the western view point. His chastity was absolute. His one big meal, taken at noon, consisted of curry and rice, and after that nothing solid. He throve on this and he became a healthy saint in body and in mind. It was with such an enduring body and mind that Gautam sat under the "Bo Tree"- the Tree of Knowledge and received enlightenment. Falling into a trance towards the wee hours of the morning one day he beheld with a kind of incandescent clarity the whole intricate concentration of cause and effect that make up the puzzle of life. He also beheld with the same clarity the path of deliverance into bliss.

The five followers that had renounced the friendship of Buddha were taken in by the holy glow that belongs to the saint's visage. Gautam became the enlightened one and preached a sermon that presented an outline of the new way of life.

Buddha's discovery under the Bo Tree was that the cause of human suffering is ignorance. We are always craving satisfaction for something we call self. But there is according to Buddha no self. We are merely transitory formations crystallized out of the general flux of things and events. We must, if we want to achieve a state of peace abandon this delusion of selfhood and the ignorant cravings that go with it. And he specified: "cravings for the gratification of passions, craving for a future life, craving for success in this life. "We must learn through the liberation of our minds from superstition, through the austere discipline of wills, and through love, to interflow with the world and be a humble and unhankering part of it. In this lies perfect peace and happiness. He advocated peace that results from understanding and passeth it.

Buddhism analyzes human existence as made up of five aggregates or "bundles" (skandhas): the material body, feelings, perceptions, predisposition's or karmic tendencies, and consciousness. A person is only a temporary combination of these aggregates, which are subject to continual change. No one remains the same for any two consecutive moments. Buddhists deny that the aggregates individually or in combination may be considered a permanent, independently existing self or soul (atman). Indeed, they regard it as a mistake to conceive of any lasting unity behind the elements that constitute an individual. Buddha held that belief such a self results in egoism, craving, and hence in suffering. Thus he taught the doctrine of anatman, or the denial of a permanent soul. He felt that all existence is characterized by the three marks of anatman (no soul), anitya (impermanence), and dukkha (suffering). The doctrine of anatman made it necessary for the Buddha to reinterpret the Indian idea of repeated rebirth in the cycle of phenomenal existence known as samsara. To this end he taught the doctrine of pratityasamutpada, or dependent origination. This 12-linked chain of causation shows how ignorance in a previous life creates the tendency for a combination of aggregates to develop. These in turn cause the mind and senses to operate. Sensations result, which lead to craving and a clinging to existence. This condition triggers the process of becoming once again, producing a renewed cycle of birth, old age, and death. Through this causal chain a connection is made between one life and the next. What is posited is a stream of renewed existence's, rather than a permanent being that moves from life to life—in effect a belief in rebirth without transmigration.

Closely related to this belief is the doctrine of karma. Karma consists of a person's acts and their ethical consequences. Human actions lead to rebirth, wherein good deeds are inevitably rewarded and evil deeds punished. Thus, neither undeserved pleasure nor unwarranted suffering exists in the world, but rather a universal justice. The karmic process operates through a kind of natural moral law rather than through a system of divine judgment. One's karma determines such matters as one's species, beauty, intelligence, longevity, wealth, and social status. According to the Buddha, karma of varying types can lead to rebirth as a human, an animal, a hungry ghost, a denizen of hell, or even one of the Hindu gods.

Although never actually denying the existence of the gods, Buddhism denies them any special role. Their lives in heaven are long and pleasurable, but they are in the same predicament as other creatures, being subject eventually to death and further rebirth in lower states of existence. They are not creators of the universe or in control of human destiny, and Buddhism denies the value of prayer and sacrifice to them. Of the possible modes of rebirth, human existence is preferable, because the deities are so engrossed in their own pleasures that they lose sight of the need for salvation. Enlightenment is possible only for humans.

The ultimate goal of the Buddhist path is release from the round of phenomenal existence with its inherent suffering. To achieve this goal is to attain nirvana, an enlightened state in which the fires of greed, hatred, and ignorance have been quenched. Not to be confused with total annihilation, nirvana is a state of consciousness beyond definition. After attaining nirvana, the enlightened individual may continue to live, burning off any remaining karma until a state of final nirvana (parinirvana) is attained at the moment of death.

In theory, the goal of nirvana is attainable by anyone, although it is a realistic goal only for members of the monastic community. In Theravada Buddhism an individual who has achieved enlightenment by following the Eightfold Path is known as an arhat, or worthy one, a type of solitary saint.

For those unable to pursue the ultimate goal, the proximate goal of better rebirth through improved karma is an option. This lesser goal is generally pursued by lay Buddhists in the hope that it will eventually lead to a life in which they are capable of pursuing final enlightenment as members of the sangha.

The ethic that leads to nirvana is detached and inner-oriented. It involves cultivating four virtuous attitudes, known as the Palaces of Brahma: loving-kindness, compassion, sympathetic joy, and equanimity. The ethic that leads to better rebirth, however, is centered on fulfilling one's duties to society. It involves acts of charity, especially support of the sangha, as well as observance of the five precepts that constitute the basic moral code of Buddhism. The precepts prohibit killing, stealing, harmful language, sexual misbehavior, and the use of intoxicants. By observing these precepts, the three roots of evil—lust, hatred, and delusion—may be overcome.

The disarming tolerance preached by Buddha is another cause of the success of Buddhism. His appeal to man's reason and experience is another important factor of his popularity. Not only must we work out our own salvation but we must think out our own creed. "Do not believe anything, because the written testimony of some ancient wise men is shown to you. . Do not believe anything on the authority of teachers or priests. Whatever accords with your own experience and after thorough investigation agrees with your reason, and is conducive to your welfare and to that of all other things, that accept as truth and live accordingly."

For two thousand five hundred years now the teachings of this man of noble penetrating vision have introduced all those who have in contact with it to a new way of life. After 45 years of missionary activity Buddha died at the age of 80 at Kusinagara in Nepal.

Lee Kuan Yew

Lee Kuan Yew the guru of Asian values is the architect of modern Singapore. He was the first prime minister of Singapore (1959-1990). Born to a wealthy Chinese family on 16 September 1923, he studied at Cambridge, England, and was admitted to the English bar in 1950. After his return he became a popular nationalist leader, and in 1954 he formed the People's Action Party. Lee was a member of the delegation that negotiated Singapore's independence from the British in 1956-58. After his party's victory in the subsequent elections, he became prime minister in 1959. Lee brought Singapore into the Federation of Malaysia in 1963, but Malay fear of Chinese domination forced Singapore to withdraw in 1965. Under his increasingly restrictive rule, the city-state became a center of international trade and relative prosperity in Asia. He resigned as prime minister in November 1990, but retained his leadership of the ruling People's Action Party.

The Japanese Occupation made Lee decide to become a politician, the communist battles turned him into a hardened politician, and separation from Malaysia provided the final drama which led to Singapore's independence, and made Lee govern it systematically.

Lee Kuan Yew's grandfather, Hoon Leong, went to an English school and began a career as a pharmacist. His fortunes improved markedly when he joined a Chinese shipping company, Heap Eng Mo Shipping Company, as a purser, making regular trips between Singapore and Indonesia. On one of these voyages, he met Ko Liem Nio in Semarang. They married and he brought her to Singapore. He moved up the company and eventually possessed power of attorney over the concerns of Sugar King Oei Tiong Ham. His fortunes rose with Oei's. By the time Kuan Yew was born, Hoon Leong was head of a wealthy family, though its fortunes suffered somewhat during the Depression of 1929 - 32. As was the practice in those days, the marriage between Lee's parents, Lee Chin Koon and Chua Jim Neo, was an arranged one. Both came from successful middle-class families and were educated in English schools.

Lee's maternal grandfather owned the former Katong market, rubber estates at Chai Chee and a row of houses next to the present Thai embassy at Orchard Road. Those days successful Chinese businessmen working within the colonial system in Singapore were able to make vast fortunes mainly in trading and property development.

The Depression took its toll and both Lee's grandfathers' wealth declined considerably. Lee's father worked first as a storekeeper at Shell, the Anglo-Dutch oil giant, and was later put in charge of various depots in Johor Bahru, Stulang and Batu Pahat. But it was his mother, Jim Neo, to whom Lee attributes much of the family's success in overcoming the financial difficulties. By then, the family had a house in Telok Kurau. For Lee and his three brothers and a sister, these were carefree days. But even though, by his own admission, he did not work very hard in school, he was always there at the top of the class. The pace quickened somewhat after he enrolled at Raffles Institution; Lee emerged top Malayan boy in the Senior Cambridge examinations. His decision to become a lawyer, which would have a profound effect on his political activities later, came about from purely pragmatic considerations. "My father and mother had friends from their wealthier days who, after the slump, were still wealthy because they had professions, either doctors or lawyers. The doctors were people like Dr Loh Poon Lip, the father of Robert Loh. The lawyer was Richard Lim Chuan Ho, who was the father of Arthur Lim, the eye surgeon. And then there was a chap called Philip Hoalim Senior. They did not become poor because they had professions. My father didn't have a profession, so he became poor and he became a storekeeper. Their message, or their moral for me, was, I'd better take a profession, or I'd run the risk of a very precarious life," Lee recapitulates.

There were three choices for a profession- medicine, law and engineering. Lee did not want to join the first two because one would have to work for a company or someone if one followed these lines. He decided to be a lawyer where one could be self employed.

These plans were shattered when Japanese forces landed at Kota Baru on the north-east coast of Malaya in the early hours of Dec 8, 1941. But the political education which followed would leave a lasting impression and change Lee's life forever. "They (the Japanese) were the masters. They swaggered around with big swords, they occupied all the big offices and the houses and the big cars and they gave the orders. So that determines who is the authority. Then, because they had the authority, they printed the money, they controlled the wealth of the country, the banks, they made the Chinese pay a $50-million tribute," Lee recalled bitterly.

Lee saw that people adjusted and they bowed, they ingratiated themselves because they had to live. Quietly, they cursed away behind the backs of the Japanese. But in the face of the Japanese, they appeared to submit and appeared to be docile. Observing this Lee learnt how power operated on people.

As time went on, food and medicine became short. Whisky, brandy, all the luxuries which could be kept in either bottles or tins—cigarettes, 555s in tins—became valuables. The people who traded with the Japanese, who pandered to their wishes, provided them with supplies, clothes, uniforms, whatever, bought these things and gave them to the officers were in favour. And some ran gambling farms in the New World and Great World. And millions of Japanese dollars were won and lost each night. They collected the money, shared it with whoever were in charge: the Japanese Kempeitai and the government or generals or whatever. They bought properties. They became very wealthy at the end of the war because the property transactions were recognized. But the notes were not.

Lee began to hate the Japanese. He did not want to learn the language. Instead he began to learn Chinese. After six months he could read Chinese fluently but the Katakana and the Hingana were alien to him. He finally registered at a Japanese school in Queen Street. After three months Lee got a job with his grandfather's old friend, a textile importer and exporter called Shimoda.

Lee worked there as a clerk, copy typist, copied the Japanese Kanji and so on. It was clerical work. But Lee saw how people had to live, they had to get rice, food, they had to feed their children. Therefore, they had to submit. It was here that Lee gained his first lesson on power and government and system and how human beings reacted. Years later Lee recalling the people and their reactions said "Some were heroic, maybe misguided. They listened to the radio, against the Japanese, they spread news, got captured by the Kempeitai, tortured. Some were just collaborators, did everything the Japanese wanted. And it was an education on human beings, human nature and human systems of government."

When the war ended, Lee had to decide between returning to Raffles College to work for the scholarship, which would fund his law studies in England or going there on his own

190

steam. Britain, land of his colonial masters and the epicenter of the vast, if fast declining Empire, might have elicited from a subservient subject of a distant outpost, 11, 000 km away, the reverence it once undoubtedly deserved.

War-torn Britain of 1946 was a different proposition altogether. For Lee, the first few months were disorienting, hectic and miserable. Arriving in October, he was already late for college admission. But being first boy in the Senior Cambridge examinations for all Malaya helped. The dean of the Law Faculty at the London School of Economics was suitably impressed and Lee found himself thrown into the rough and tumble of undergraduate life in the imperial capital, an experience he found thoroughly unpleasant.

With the help of some friends in Cambridge and a sympathetic Censor of Fitzwilliam House, he got himself admitted and moved to the university town. Lee went on to distinguish himself in Cambridge, obtaining a rare double first. But though his top priority was his studies, something else much more intense was stirring in him.

It was in England that he began to seriously question the continued right of the British to govern Singapore. The Japanese Occupation had demonstrated in a way nothing else could have done that the British were not a superior people with a God-given right to govern. What he saw of them during those four years in Britain convinced him even more of this. They were in it for their own benefit, and he read all about this in their own newspapers. "Why should they run this place for your benefit? And when it comes tumbling down, I'm the chap who suffers. That, I think, was the start of it all, "recalled Lee.

"At that time, it was also the year following my stay in England and insurgency had started (in Malaya) and I had also seen the communist Malayan People's Anti-Japanese Army (MPAJA) marching on the streets. "I would say Japanese

Occupation, one year here, seeing MPAJA and seeing the British trying to re-establish their administration, not very adept . . . I mean the old mechanisms had gone and the old habits of obedience and respect had also gone because people had seen them run away."

The Japanese packed up. Women and children, those who could get away, did. The local population was supposed to panic when the bombs fell, but they panicked more than the locals. Thus the old order gave way to new The old relationship no longer existed.

Lee saw Britain and he saw the British people as they were. And whilst he met nothing but consideration and a certain benevolence from people at the top, at the bottom, when he had to deal with landladies and the shopkeepers, it was pretty rough. They treated him as a colonial and Lee resented that. Lee resented that the white men and women in inferior position socially should be governing him. He decided to put an end to that.

As one of the first-generation leaders who fought the colonial powers to gain independence for his country, Lee understood the forces and the motivation that had driven them to action. He knew only too well the force of circumstances and the uncertain temper of the times that had thrown up these men. What may surprise the modern reader is how early in Lee's political career he came to this conclusion. The problem did not suddenly dawn on him in the twilight of his political career, when succession became a pressing issue. When he spoke of it in 1966, barely one year into Singapore's independence, almost the entire Old Guard leadership was relatively young and intact. Perhaps even more surprising is that in an interview 30 years ago, he had already identified one core aspect of the problem which in the '90s received much attention of improving the incentives for young men and women to join the government. "I would say the real problem now in Singapore politically is - as different from the economics of it - is how do we, over the next 10 years, allow a new generation to emerge to take over from us? This is important. We are not getting younger. We cannot go on forever. And you must allow sufficient free play on the ground for a new generation to emerge well in time to take over. My problem is there are so many career opportunities now that unless we do something to make politics more attractive incentive-wise, your best men are going into executive and managerial careers. This will leave your second-best careerist . . . " (July 1966)

Lee tackled these problems with the typical Lee approach to governance. He believed the problem was especially acute for newly-emerging nations; developed ones already had an established tradition for throwing up leaders. Yet, it was the newly-independent countries that cried out for capable leaders to solve their numerous and pressing problems. "Being confronted with this problem myself, I have often asked: "How do we ensure succession?' - not on the basis of "I like A and therefore I groom A for leadership.' Unless you want long periods of anarchy and chaos, you have to create a self-continuing—not a self-perpetuating—but a self-continuing power structure. " Lee's wisdom and insight into the kernel of the problem made him a successful leader.

Making Singapore a garden city was an obsession with him. As with the man who has been at Singapore's helm for 38 years, 31 of which he served as prime minister, his approach to the problem has been typically hardheaded and pragmatic. For him, the object of the exercise was not all about smelling roses. In the end it was about keeping Singapore ahead of the competition. A well kept garden, he would say, is a daily effort, and would demonstrate to outsiders the people's ability to organize and to be systematic. "The grass has got to be mown every other day, the trees have to be tended, the flowers in the gardens have to be looked after so they know this place gives attention to detail." When Lee Kuan Yew decided to make Singapore a garden city, to soften the harshness of life in one of the world's most densely populated countries, he did not write a memorandum to the environment minister or to the head of the agency responsible for parks and trees. He did not form a committee nor seek outside help to hire the best landscapists money could buy. For one thing, in the 1960s, when he was thinking of these matters, money was in short supply. In fact, having been unceremoniously booted out of Malaysia, the country's economic survival was hanging in the balance. For another, there was no environment minister to speak of then, so low down in the list of priorities were these matters. When jobs had to be created and communists fought in the streets, only the birds were interested in flowers and trees.

Lee sought pragmatic solutions to realize his dreams. Fertilizers would replenish the soil, and so began the task of making compost from rubbish dumps, adding calcium, and lime where the ground was too acidic. Years later, when economic survival was no longer an issue and Singapore's success was acknowledged worldwide, he was still working to make the garden city possible. When expressways and flyovers sprouted all over the island, he had officials look for plants which could survive below the flyovers where the sun seldom shone. And instead of having to water these plants regularly, which was costly, he got them to devise a way to channel water from the roads, after filtering it to get rid of the oil and grime from the traffic above.

The constant search for solutions would not end. When development intensified even further and the roads and flyovers became broader still, shutting out the light completely from the plants below, he did not give up. The road was split into two so there would be a gap in the middle with enough space for sunshine and rain to seep through and greenery and vegetation to thrive below. "I sent them on missions all along the Equator and the tropical, subtropical zones, looking for new types of trees, plants, creepers and so on. From Africa, the Caribbean, Latin, Middle, Central America, we've come back with new plants. It's a very small sum. But if you get the place greened up, if you get all those creepers up, you take away the heat, you'll have a different city," he said.

Today plainclothes security officers tread the narrow carpeted corridors of Lee Kuan's office, buzzing each other periodically over their walkie-talkies. In a brightly lit room, a secretary works at her computer, one ear peeled to an intercom linking her to an adjoining office where Lee Kuan Yew works. It is an L-shaped room with an attached bathroom. It is free of personal paraphemalia. No family photographs decorate his table, no personal mementoes line his walls. Lee sits behind a desk, his back to a computer. He is about 1. 8 meters tall, and slim. His trousers, which are usually in light hues, are loose, and he tugs at the waistband frequently. He is at least 10 kilograms lighter than when he was in his forties. His shirts are well-pressed though well-worn, and he wears a windbreaker, usually beige, when he is in the office.

At 74, his hair is white. The once wiry black mop has thinned considerably over the years, accentuating a broad, high forehead under which small, piercing eyes stare. His face is pink in tone, the skin mostly unlined, though tiny creases crisscross the skin on his eyelids. His nails are neatly trimmed. A low cabinet next to it is stacked with books and files. A wood-panelled wall camouflages the door to the room where his two secretaries work. A teak table for eight stands four meters from his desk, a jade dragon jar in the middle. Lee works in this office six days a week, from about 10 in the morning to 6:30 in the evening, when he puts his work aside for his daily exercise in the Istana grounds. He has been known to come back to the office on Sundays and public holidays.

Even in a private setting, he is a forceful personality. His facial expression changes quickly and his hands often chop the air to emphasize a point. His voice rises and falls according to his emotions. He is quick to show impatience, and slow to smile. He has never suffered fools lightly. This is the man who has more than anyone else shaped the history of modern Singapore. Today, he stands an inspiration to the older generation as well as the new generation. He stands tall and straight an example worth emulating.

Confucius

Confucius was a Chinese philosopher. He was one of the most influential figures in Chinese history. He lived between 551 BC to 479 BC. Though he died centuries before, his teachings and philosophy gave birth to a movement, "Confucianism", that lives on even today. In recent China, the stature of God was nearly granted to him. This would indeed have amused Confucius had he been living today because the he did not overly concern himself with religion. He said, "Respect the spirits, but keep them at a distance."

Confucius was born in the state of Lu (present-day Shandong [Shantung] Province) of the noble K'ung clan. His original name was K'ung Ch'iu. His father, commander of a district in Lu, died three years after Confucius was born, leaving the family in poverty; but Confucius nevertheless received a fine education. At an early age he displayed remarkable mental ability. Although he had to work for a living his interest in education and the quest of knowledge never waned. At the age of fifteen the thought of becoming a sage entered his mind. He was married at the age of 19 and had one son and two daughters.

During the four years immediately after his marriage, poverty compelled him to perform menial labors for the chief of the district. His mother died in 527 BC, and after a period of mourning he began his career as a teacher, usually traveling about and instructing the small body of disciples that had gathered around him. His fame as a man of learning and character and his reverence for Chinese ideals and customs soon spread through the principality of Lu. At the age of twenty two he founded an academy in which the principles of right conduct and government were taught. Both, the rich and the poor attended his school. He charged high fees from the rich and did not turn away the poor on account of their poverty. Confucius displayed unusual administrative capabilities. He was not deterred to do away with the old established way of life. If required, he was quite willing to experiment with the new.

Living as he did in the second half of the Zhou (Chou) dynasty (1027?-256 BC), when feudalism degenerated in China and intrigue and vice were rampant, Confucius deplored the contemporary disorder and lack of moral standards. He came to believe that the only remedy was to convert people once more to the principles and precepts of the sages of antiquity. He therefore lectured to his pupils on the ancient classics. He taught the great value of the power of example. Rulers, he said, can be great only if they themselves lead exemplary lives, and were they willing to be guided by moral principles, their states would inevitably become prosperous and happy.

During these years he came in contact with the famous spiritualist leader Lao-tsze. He was much impressed with Lao, though he did not really believe in the philosophy propounded by Lao. As time went by Confucius gained many followers. His lessons were gathered from everyday life. A sudden revolution in the state of Lu caused the lord to flee and Confucius too followed the lord into exile. Passing with his disciples by the mountain T'ai he saw a woman wailing. On inquiring the reason for her grief the woman said, "My husband's father was killed at this spot by a tiger, my husband too met the same fate and now my son has been killed by the tiger. "Asked why she did not leave the place she replied because the government was not oppressive. Quick to point out a moral Confucius said, "Remember this my children, an oppressive government is fiercer and more feared than a tiger."

Confucius had, however, no opportunity to put his theories to a public test until, at the age of 50, he was appointed magistrate of Chung-tu, and the next year minister of crime of the state of Lu. His administration was successful; reforms were introduced, justice was fairly dispensed, and crime was almost eliminated. So powerful did Lu become, that the ruler of a neighboring state maneuvered to secure the minister's dismissal. Confucius left his office in 496 BC, traveling about and teaching, vainly hoping that some other prince would allow him to undertake measures of reform. In 484 BC, after a fruitless search for an ideal ruler, he returned for the last time to Lu. He spent the remaining years of his life in retirement, writing commentaries on the classics. He died in Lu at the age of seventy one and was buried in a tomb at Ch'ü-fu, Shandong.

Confucius did not put into writing the principles of his philosophy; these were handed down only through his disciples. The Lun Yü (Analects), a work compiled by some of his disciples, is considered the most reliable source of information about his life and teachings. One of the historical works that he is said to have compiled and edited, the Ch'un Ch'iu (Spring and Autumn Annals), is an annalistic account of Chinese history in the state of Lu from 722 to 481 BC. In learning he wished to be known as a transmitter rather than as a creator, and he therefore revived the study of the ancient books. His own teachings, together with those of his main disciples, are found in the Shih Shu (Four Books) of Confucian literature, which became the textbooks of later Chinese generations. Confucius was greatly venerated during his lifetime and in succeeding ages. Although he himself had little belief in the supernatural, he has been revered almost as a spiritual being by millions.

The entire teaching of Confucius was practical and ethical, rather than religious. He claimed to be a restorer of ancient morality and held that proper outward acts based on the five virtues of kindness, uprightness, decorum, wisdom, and faithful ess constitute the whole of human duty. Reverence for parents, living and dead, was one of his key concepts. His view of government was paternalistic, and he enjoined all individuals to observe carefully their duties toward the state. In subsequent centuries his teachings exerted a powerful influence on the Chinese nation.

Confucianism has influenced the Chinese attitude toward life, set the patterns of living and standards of social value, and provided the background for Chinese political theories and institutions. It has spread from China to Korea, Japan, and Vietnam and has aroused interest among Western scholars.

Although Confucianism became the official ideology of the Chinese state, it has never existed as an established religion with a church and priesthood. Chinese scholars honoured Confucius as a great teacher and sage but did not worship him as a personal god. Nor did Confucius himself ever claim divinity. Unlike Christian churches, the temples built to Confucius were not places in which organized community groups gathered to worship, but public edifices designed for annual ceremonies, especially on the philosopher's birthday. Several attempts to deify Confucius and to proselyte Confucianism failed because of the essentially secular nature of the philosophy.

The principles of Confucianism are contained in the nine ancient Chinese works handed down by Confucius and his followers, who lived in an age of great philosophic activity. These writings can be divided into two groups: the Five Classics and the Four Books.

The Wu Ching (Five Classics), which originated before the time of Confucius, consist of the I Ching (Book of Changes), Shu Ching (Book of History), Shih Ching (Book of Poetry), Li Chi (Book of Rites), and Ch'un Ch'iu (Spring and Autumn Annals). The I Ching is a manual of divination probably compiled before the 11th century BC; its supplementary philosophical portion, contained in a series of appendixes, may have been written later by Confucius and his disciples. The Shu Ching is a collection of ancient historical documents, and the Shih Ching, an anthology of ancient poems. The Li Chi deals with the principles of conduct, including those for public and private ceremonies; it was destroyed in the 3rd century BC, but presumably much of its material was preserved in a later compilation, the Record of Rites. The Ch'un Ch'iu, the only work reputedly compiled by Confucius himself, is a chronicle of major historical events in feudal China from the 8th century BC to Confucius's death early in the 5th century BC.

The Shih Shu (Four Books), compilations of the sayings of Confucius and Mencius and of commentaries by followers on their teachings, are the Lun Yü (Analects), a collection of maxims by Confucius that form the basis of his moral and political philosophy; Ta Hsüeh (The Great Learning) and Chung Yung (The Doctrine of the Mean), containing some of

Confucius's philosophical utterances arranged systematically with comments and expositions by his disciples; and the Mencius (Book of Mencius), containing the teachings of one of Confucius's great followers.

The keynote of Confucian ethics is jen, variously translated as "love," "goodness," "humanity," and "human-heartedness. " Jen is a supreme virtue representing human qualities at their best. In human relations, construed as those between one person and another, jen is manifested in chung, or faithfulness to oneself and others, and shu, or altruism, best expressed in the Confucian golden rule, "Do not do to others what you do not want done to yourself. "Other important Confucian virtues include righteousness, propriety, integrity, and filial piety. One who possesses all these virtues becomes a chün-tzu (perfect gentleman). Politically, Confucius advocated a paternalistic government in which the sovereign is benevolent and honorable and the subjects are respectful and obedient. The ruler should cultivate moral perfection in order to set a good example to the people. In education Confucius upheld the theory, remarkable for the feudal period in which he lived, that "in education, there is no class distinction."

After the death of Confucius two major schools of Confucian thought emerged: one was represented by Mencius, the other by Hsün-tzu (Hsün K'uang, 300?-235? BC). Mencius continued the ethical teachings of Confucius by stressing the innate goodness of human nature. He believed, however, that original human goodness can become depraved through one's own destructive effort or through contact with an evil environment. The problem of moral cultivation is therefore to preserve or at least to restore the goodness that is one's birthright. In political thought, Mencius is sometimes considered one of the early advocates of democracy, for he advanced the idea of the people's supremacy in the state.

In opposition to Mencius, Hsün-tzu contended that a person is born with an evil nature but that it can be regenerated through moral education. He believed that desires should be guided and restrained by the rules of propriety and that character should be molded by an orderly observance of rites and by the practice of music. This code serves as a powerful influence on character by properly directing emotions and by providing inner harmony. Hsün-tzu was the main exponent of ritualism in Confucianism.

After a brief period of eclipse in the 3rd century BC, Confucianism was revived during the Han dynasty (206 BC-AD 220). The Confucian works, copies of which had been destroyed in the preceding period, were restored to favour, canonized, and taught by learned scholars in national academies. The works also formed the basis of later civil service examinations; candidates for responsible government positions received their appointments on the strength of their knowledge of classic literature. As a result, Confucianism secured a firm hold on Chinese intellectual and political life.

The success of Han Confucianism was attributable to Tung Chung-shu, who first recommended a system of education built upon the teachings of Confucius. Tung Chung-shu believed in a close correspondence between human beings and nature; thus a person's deeds, especially those of the sovereign, are often responsible for unusual phenomena in nature. Because of the sovereign's authority, he or she is to blame for such phenomena as fire, flood, earthquake, and eclipse. Because these ill omens can descend on earth as a warning to humanity that all is not well in this world, the fear of heavenly punishment proves useful as a curb to the monarch's absolute power.

In the political chaos that followed the fall of the Han dynasty, Confucianism was overshadowed by the rival philosophies of Taoism and Buddhism, and the philosophy suffered a temporary setback. Nevertheless, the Confucian Classics continued to be the chief source of learning for scholars, and with the restoration of peace and prosperity in the Tang dynasty (618-907), the spread of Confucianism was encouraged. The monopoly of learning by Confucian scholars once again ensured them the highest bureaucratic positions. Confucianism returned as an orthodox state teaching.

The intellectual activities of the Song (Sung) dynasty (960-1279) gave rise to a new system of Confucian thought based on a mixture of Buddhist and Taoist elements; the new school of Confucianism was known as Neo-Confucianism. The scholars who evolved this intellectual system were themselves well versed in the other two philosophies. Although primarily teachers of ethics, they were also interested in the theories of the universe and the origin of human nature.

Neo-Confucianism branched out into two schools of philosophy. The foremost exponent of one school was Chu Hsi, an eminent thinker second only to Confucius and Mencius in prestige, who established a new philosophical foundation for the teachings of Confucianism by organizing scholarly opinion into a cohesive system. According to the Neo-Confucianist system Chu Hsi represented, all objects in nature are composed of two inherent forces: li, an immaterial universal principle or law; and ch'i, the substance of which all material things are made. Whereas ch'i may change and dissolve, li, the underlying law of the myriad things, remains constant and indestructible. Chu Hsi further identifies the li in humankind with human nature, which is essentially the same for all people. The phenomenon of particular differences can be attributed to the varying proportions and densities of the ch'i found among individuals. Thus, those who receive a ch'i that is turbid will find their original nature obscured and should cleanse their nature to restore its purity. Purity can be achieved by extending one's knowledge of the li in each individual object. When, after much sustained effort, one has investigated and comprehended the universal li or natural law inherent in all animate and inanimate objects, one becomes a sage.

Opposed to the li (law) school is the hsin (mind) school of Neo-Confucianism. The chief exponent of the hsin school was Wang Yang-ming, who taught the unity of knowledge and practice. His major proposition was that "apart from the mind, neither law nor object" exists. In the mind, he asserted, are embodied all the laws of nature, and nothing exists without the mind. One's supreme effort should be to develop "the intuitive knowledge" of the mind, not through the study or investigation of natural law, but through intense thought and calm meditation.

During the Qing (Ch'ing) dynasty (1644-1911) there was a strong reaction to both the li and hsin schools of Neo-Confucian thought. Qing scholars advocated a return to the earlier and supposedly more authentic Confucianism of the Han period, when it was still unadulterated by Buddhist and Taoist ideas. They developed textual criticism of the Confucian Classics based on scientific methodology, using philology, history, and archaeology to reinforce their scholarship. In addition, scholars such as Tai Chen introduced an empiricist point of view into Confucian philosophy.

Toward the end of the 19th century the reaction against Neo-Confucian metaphysics took a different turn. Instead of confining themselves to textual studies, Confucian scholars took an active interest in politics and formulated reform programs based on Confucian doctrine. K'ang Yu-wei, a leader of the Confucian reform movement, made an attempt to exalt the philosophy as a national religion. Because of foreign threats to China and the urgent demand for drastic political measures, the reform movements failed; in the intellectual confusion that followed the Chinese revolution of 1911, Confucianism was branded as decadent and reactionary. With the collapse of the monarchy and the traditional family structure, from which much of its strength and support was derived, Confucianism lost its hold on the nation. In the past, it often had managed to weather adversities and to emerge with renewed vigour, but during this period of unprecedented social upheavals it lost its previous ability to adapt to changing circumstances.

Confucius continues to be revered as China's greatest teacher; Confucian classics are studied, and Confucian virtues, embodied for countless generations in the familiar sayings and common-sense wisdom of the Chinese people, will remain the cornerstone of ethics. Although the Chinese Communist victory of 1949 underlined the uncertain future of Confucianism. Many Confucian-based traditions were put aside. The family system, for example, much revered in the past as a central Confucian institution, was de-emphasized. Few Confucian classics were published, and official campaigns against Confucianism were organized in the late 1960s and early '70s. But as a great ancient sage Confucius will live on.

Confucius' tomb outside the city of K'iuh-fow, on a lush green hill midst the cypress tress is an apt place for this "most sagely teacher: all accomplished, all- informed king. "The marble statue of this wise man looks on as generations of Chinese come to pay their homage to their master who taught them to tread the path that was right-always.

Nelson Mandela

Mandela, Nelson Rolihlahla the South African activist, statesman, and Nobel laureate, is the first elected black president of South Africa. He was elected in 1994. Mandela rose to national prominence as the leader of protest against the white minority government's policy of rigid racial segregation known as apartheid, which officially ended in 1991. . The word apartheid means "separateness" in the Africans language and it describes the rigid racial division between the governing white minority population and the nonwhite majority population. The National Party introduced apartheid as part of their campaign in the 1948 elections, and with the National Party victory, apartheid became the governing political policy for South Africa until the early 1990s. During this time under the able leadership of the Nelson Mandela and F. D Clerk aparthied came to an end.

South Africa had a long history of Aparthied. Mandela grew up midst this retrictive regime where the apartheid laws classified people according to three major racial groups—white; Bantu, or black Africans; and Coloured, or people of mixed descent. Later Asians, or Indians and Pakistanis, were added as a fourth category. The laws determined where members of each group could live, what jobs they could hold, and what type of education they could receive. Laws prohibited most social contact between races, authorized segregated public facilities, and denied any representation of nonwhites in the national government. People who openly opposed apartheid were considered communists and the government passed strict security legislation which in effect turned South Africa into a police state. This racial injustice left a deep impact on Mandela. When he was elected president in the country's first democratic elections, Mandela promised a new multiracial government that would work to reverse the economic and social problems caused by apartheid.

Mandela was born in 1918 as the son of a Tembu tribal chief in Umtata, in what is now the province of Eastern Cape. He became a lawyer, and in 1944 joined the African National Congress (ANC), a civil rights group, and helped establish the organization's Youth League. In 1956 Mandela went on trial for treason, but was acquitted in 1961. During this time he married Nkosikazi Nomzamo Madikizela (Winnie); She was a South African political activist, known for advocating militant resistance to apartheid. She was trained as a medical social worker. When he was convicted and sentenced to life imprisonment in 1964, she continued his work of the ANC. She herself was imprisoned and held in solitary confinement from 1969 to 1970. In 1976 Mandela was declared a banned person and was ordered to restrict her movements, but she defied these orders.

Mandela was implicated in 1988 when members of the Mandela United Football Club (who served as her bodyguards) beat four young black men, one of whom died in the Mandela home. She was cited in 1990 for complicity in the murder and was convicted of kidnapping in 1991. In 1992, after new evidence surfaced regarding these and other charges, Mandela resigned her position as head of the ANC's social welfare department. In addition, she was stripped of a regional position in the ANC's Women's League and gave up her seat on the ANC's National Executive Committee. Mandela unsuccessfully appealed her kidnapping conviction in 1993. The court, however, waived her prison term and instead ordered her to pay fines. In December 1993, despite her criminal conviction and her public criticisms of ANC leadership, Mandela regained her position as president of the ANC's Women's League.

In 1990 Nelson Mandela was released from prison after the ban on the ANC was lifted. In April 1992 he announced that he and his wife were separating. In May 1994 Nelson Mandela, the newly elected president of South Africa, appointed her deputy minister of arts, culture, science, and technology, a post she held until April 1995, when she resigned due to ongoing conflicts with Mandela and his administration. The Mandelas were divorced in March 1996.

In the early 1960s Mandela led the ANC's paramilitary wing, Umkhonto we Sizwe ("Spear of the Nation"). Arrested again in August 1962, he was sentenced to five years in prison. While in prison, Mandela, along with several others, was convicted of sabotage and treason and in June 1964 was sentenced to life imprisonment. During this period Mandela became a worldwide symbol of resistance to white domination in South Africa. The government, under President F. W. de Klerk, released Mandela in February 1990 after lifting the ban on the ANC. Mandela assumed leadership of the ANC and led negotiations with the government for a new constitution that would grant political power to the country's black majority population. In 1991 the government repealed the last of the laws that formed the legal basis for apartheid. Mandela and de Klerk shared the 1993 Nobel Peace Prize for their efforts in establishing democracy and racial harmony in South Africa. In May 1994, after the country's first multiracial elections, Mandela became president of South Africa.

The decision to bring an end to apartheid caused many whites to defect to more conservative parties. In failing health, Botha resigned in 1989. F. W. de. Klerk, his successor, continued the policy of eliminating apartheid. Calling for a negotiated settlement of South Africa's racial and political problems, in February 1990 de Klerk ended a 30-year ban on the ANC and released its leader, Nelson Mandela, from prison. The negotiation process proved to be long and difficult. De Klerk's Nationalist Party was unwilling at first to transfer rule completely to the country's black majority, and tried vigorously to institute minority veto power over majority decisions. The ANC then staged general strikes and other nonviolent protests to try to force the Nationalists to change their position on this issue. Eventually, as a result of compromises on both sides, an agreement was reached on November 13, 1993. This agreement pledged to institute a nonracial, nonsexist, unified, and democratic South Africa based on the principle of "one person, one vote. " Multiracial elections were scheduled for April 1994. A Transitional Executive Council was formed to supervise the elections, which would install new national and provincial governments.

In March 1994, Lucas Mangope, the leader of the bantustan of Bophuthatswana, protesting the dissolution of the bantustans under the interim constitution, declared that Bophuthatswana would not participate in the elections. Bophuthatswana citizens, eager to vote in the elections, protested, while armed white extremists, opposed to the changes occurring in the country, came to assist Mangope. Bophuthatswana civil servants and soldiers then rioted for four days until Mangope agreed to allow participation in the elections. Meanwhile, the Zulu-dominated Inkatha Freedom Party refused to participate in the elections until an agreement was reached regarding the status of the Zulu territory and the Zulu king. Inkatha did finally participate, with the condition that mediated talks with the government would take place after the elections. Despite pre-election turmoil, the elections were held at the end of April in relative calm and order. The ANC scored a clear victory, and Mandela was inaugurated as the country's first black president on May 10, 1994. In June South Africa rejoined the Commonwealth of Nations.

Also that month, the government established the Truth and Reconciliation Commission to investigate human-rights abuses during the apartheid era. The commission decided that those who admitted to committing political crimes would be pardoned and those who remained silent could be prosecuted. Although the stated purpose of the commission was not to punish but to help the country come to terms with its past, the commission's role was a subject of debate. While some sought punishment for crimes committed, others feared that the functionaries and not the commanders would be held responsible for the apartheid crimes. In November 1995 Mandela selected Archbishop Desmond. M. Tutu to serve as head of the commission.

In February 1995 representatives of the Inkatha Freedom Party in parliament threatened to abandon their seats because the mediated talks promised in 1994 had not taken place. Inkatha advocated more autonomy for the provinces than the interim constitution provided. Inkatha members did withdraw from parliament in April. A related topic of disagreement between Inkatha and the government was whether the central government or provincial governments should pay the salaries of traditional leaders. The Inkatha-led government of the province of Kwa Zulu-Natal wanted to pay Zulu chiefs, who form an important part of Inkatha's power base. In December 1995, however, Mandela signed into law a bill that allows the central government to pay traditional leaders. Inkatha representatives remained absent from parliament in May 1996 when the new constitution was ratified.

Mandela's fight for the civil rights of the Blacks in South Africa and his resistance to white domination is an inspiration to all people across the globe. His patience, resilience of spirit and his able administration as President of South Africa has made him a living legend.

Carl Jung

Carl Jung was a Swiss psychiatrist, who founded the analytical school of psychology. Jung broadened Sigmund Freud's psychoanalytical approach, interpreting mental and emotional disturbances as an attempt to find personal and spiritual wholeness.

Born on July 26, 1875, in Kesswil, Switzerland, the son of a Protestant clergyman, Jung developed during his lonely childhood an inclination for dreaming and fantasy that greatly influenced his adult work. He studied in a school near Basel where the elite Germans studied. The social class difference between Jung's humble origins and his more sophisticated friends became apparent. Years later Jung recalled, "For the first time I became aware that I was a poor parson's son who had holes in his shoes. Although he did well in school he never did really like to attend it. He however had difficulty in mathematics and physical education. One day at school he was knocked down by some boys in the street. His head hit a kerbstone. He recovered but was prone to fainting spells, specially whenever he had to attend school. This behaviour continued until he heard his father confide in a friend that he had now hardly any money left to spend on Carl's medical aid. This opened Carl's eyes and he realized the inconvenience he was causing everyone. This was also the turning point in his life. It got him interested in human behaviour and psychology. Carl later recalled, "That is when I learnt what neurosis is."

After graduating in medicine in 1902 from the universities of Basel and Zürich, with a wide background in biology, zoology, paleontology, and archaeology, he began his work on word association, in which a patient's responses to stimulus words revealed what Jung called "complexes"—a term that has since become universal. Psychiatry interested him because it combined human behaviour and science. In December 1900, the young doctor became a staff physician at Zurich's Burgholzli Psychiatric Hospital. He applied the method of free association that lent him an insight into the repressed complexes in a person.

These studies brought him international renown and led him to a close collaboration with Freud. With the publication of Psychology of the Unconscious (1912; trans. 1916), however, Jung declared his independence from Freud's narrowly sexual interpretation of the libido by showing the close parallels between ancient myths and psychotic fantasies and by explaining human motivation in terms of a larger creative energy. He gave up the presidency of the International Psychoanalytic Society and founded a movement called analytical psychology. Jung started to practice at his home in the village of Kusnacht on the shore of the Lake of Zurich. He received patients from all over the world. He abandoned Freud's "couch therapy" in which the patient lay on the couch and talked endlessly without interruption from the doctor, who just took noted and made terse judgements. Jung, instead sat across from his patients:"I confront the patient as one human being to another. Analysis is a dialogue demanding two partners; the doctor has something to say but so has the patient."

Jung's work with the lesser known realm of the unconscious made him a success with the patients. His patient listening to the words and sentences uttered by the mentally ill enabled him to treat them. His success amongst the psychiatrists of the day was phenomenal. He wrote more than 30 books and hundreds of articles on the unconscious.

Like Freud he believed in the power dreams to interpret the workings of the unconcious. Dreams symbolized ignored or rejected aspects of our own personality.

Jung journeyed around the world and studied various religions and myths. He asked people to report their dreams in the most minute detail. He was astonished to observe that across cultural barriers people's dreams were similar. They showed the appearance of repeated motifs." just as the body shows a common anatomy over and above all racial differences, so too the human psyche possesses a common substratum transcending all differences in culture and conciousness." Jung named this the "collective unconciousness." He later made a distinction between the personal unconscious, or the repressed feelings and thoughts developed during an individual's life, and the collective unconscious, or those inherited feelings, thoughts, and memories shared by all humanity. The collective unconscious, according to Jung, is made up of what he called "archetypes," or primordial images. These correspond to such experiences as confronting death or choosing a mate and manifest themselves symbolically in religions, myths, fairy tales, and fantasies.

According to Jung there were two kinds of dreams: the "big" ones and the "little" ones. The "big" dreams were the ones with poetic force and beauty that occurred mostly during the critical stages of life such as puberty, onset of middleage and within sight of death. The "little" dreams were about everyday occurances. Jung put a lot of premium to the quality and the contents of the dreams. Dreams he observed often directed and tried to convey important messages to the people. They must he felt learn to listen and interpret correctly.

Towards the end of his life when Jung was in his 86th year he dreamt of a more beautiful version of his second home, the beloved "tower" at Bollingen, bathed in radiant light. a voice told him that it was now finished and ready for him. He also saw that as he wandered down to the shore of the lake, he saw a mother wolverine teaching her pup to swim. Jung believed this was a clear message to prepare himself for death-the transition to another state as unfamiliar to him as water was to the young wolverine.

Perhaps the best compliment that Jung received in his lifetime was from the victims of Second World War, who haunted by the horrors of the war could lead normal lives until the therapy of Carl Jung purged and they started life a new. Explorer and author Laurens van der Post was a similar victim of the war. At his wife's urgings he met Carl Jung whom he thought would be a pompous scholar with little compassion in him. But instead he confronted a captivating man, bubbling with energy. As they talked his "feelings of isolation and loneliness" from the years of imprisonment in a Japanese prisoner-of-war camp "vanished". Jung's healing touch had cured Post as nothing else had and he said, "I have known many of those the world considers great, but Carl Jung is almost the only one of whose greatness I am certain. "

During his remaining 50 years Jung developed his theories, drawing on a wide knowledge of mythology and history; travels to diverse cultures in New Mexico, India, and Kenya; and especially the dreams and fantasies of his childhood. In 1921 he published a major work, Psychological Types (trans. 1923), in which he dealt with the relationship between the conscious and unconscious and proposed the now well-known personality types, extrovert and introvert.

Jung's therapeutic approach aimed at reconciling the diverse states of personality, which he saw divided not only into the opposites of introvert and extrovert, but also into those of sensing and intuiting, and of feeling and thinking. By understanding how the personal unconscious integrates with the collective unconscious, Jung theorized, a patient can achieve a state of individuation, or wholeness of self.

Jung wrote voluminously, especially on analytical methods and the relationships between psychotherapy and religious belief. Books like the Modern Man in Search of a Soul, Memories, Dreams, Reflections continue to fascinate the reader even today. They present him with the richness of Jung's mind. As a review in the New York times declared, "People are reading Jung now because his concern are theirs. The lifelong search for meaning and wholeness that Jung recounts is one they too are embarked on."

He died on June 6, 1961, in Küsnacht.

Suharto

Suharto the, second president of Indonesia, born in 1921 in Yogyakarta. He attended a Dutch-run military academy, but later fought against the Dutch and gradually rose through the military ranks to become a major general in 1962. In 1963 he was put in charge of the army strategic command, a special force kept on alert in case of emergencies, and he was instrumental in thwarting the attempted coup in 1965. When President Sukarno, in the aftermath of that effort, acted indecisively, he was forced to cede power to the military, and Suharto took over; he was named acting president in 1967, elected to a full term in 1968, and reelected in 1973, 1978, 1983, 1988, and 1993. After purging Indonesia of Communist influence, Suharto's authoritarian regime sought to provide a stable climate for economic growth based on petroleum revenues. The economy was strong until recently and Suharto due to charges of corruption and the failing economy had to step down as President.

For three decades the unchallenged ruler of one of Asia's most populous countries. Boosted his international profile by heading the Non-Aligned Movement, chairing a conference on Cambodian peace and hosting an Asia Pacific Economic Cooperation summit. Called the "Father of Development" for revitalizing the debt-ridden economy he took over from Sukarno. Skilled at keeping the military happy and opponents weak. Critics fault his unwillingness to plan an orderly succession.

Most Indonesians have known no president but Suharto. He maneuvered to power in 1966, after the chaos of a communist coup attempt and a purge in which hundreds of thousands died. He has ruled, some would say reigned, without a serious challenge ever since. Suharto created a New Order for the vast archipelago, and recreated himself as a new kind of Javanese king. He was until recently, the paramount leader, the sole arbiter of policy, in a country that is now home to nearly 200 million people.

Suharto has built a political system on unity and consensus. He has been selected president by a 1,000-member assembly six times — and he has never faced a challenger. To understand the nature of Suharto's control consider this description of a traditional Javanese leader by political scientist Benedict Anderson: "The man of power should have to exert himself as little as possible. The slightest lifting of his finger should be able to set a chain of actions in motion."

Suharto's fingers extended from Jakarta to the most remote village. He approved every general, appointed every governor. He hand-picked the heads of the army, navy, airforce and police. He had the power of veto promotions to key command posts. Suharto had the final say over more than half of the seats in the 1,000-member assembly that selected the president every five years. His eldest daughter Siti Hardiyanti Rukmana was chairwoman of the central board of ruling party, Golkar. One son controlled a huge Indonesian conglomerate; another had the rights to build the national car.

As president he traveled throughout Indonesia to open factories and talk to farmers. But he rarely explained the details of his policies. His critics become enemies. The government then tried to co-operate and weaken them. That's precisely what happened to Megawati Sukarnoputri, the daughter of Indonesia's founding president Sukarno. When she began gaining prominence as leader of the opposition Indonesian Democratic Party, the government contrived to oust her.

No president, no prime minister, no tycoon in recent times could match the power of Suharto. Many believed, until recently that he intended to die in office — or that he would remain only until he cuts a deal with the army to protect his children's wealth. As Anderson pointing out, for Suharto, as for the ancient Javanese kings said, "Power is neither legitimate nor illegitimate. Power is."

Under Sukarno's Guided Democracy (1959-1965), Indonesia pursued an active foreign policy, demanding that the Netherlands surrender West Irian (which, following a brief period of UN administration, was finally turned over to Indonesia in 1963) and opposing the formation of the Federation of Malaysia in 1963. Domestically, the economic decline continued, and both the army and the Communists (Partai Komunis Indonesia, or PKI) increased their power, with tension growing between the two groups.

The situation culminated in a coup attempt on September 30, 1965, led by Lieutenant Colonel Untung of the palace guard, in which six top generals were brutally murdered. General Suharto, head of the army's strategic command, suppressed the coup attempt, took control of the army, and eventually maneuvered Sukarno into handing over effective power to him in March 1966. Although the identity and motives of the prime instigators of the coup attempt remain a subject of controversy, the army alleged PKI responsibility; during late 1965, despite Sukarno's efforts to moderate the situation, army units and some Muslim groups, particularly in the countryside, began massacring Communists and their supporters. Estimates of the number killed range between 300, 000 and 1 million. The PKI was banned on March 13, 1966, and the government arrested hundreds of thousands of people accused of involvement in the coup attempt. The last of these prisoners have yet to be released, and there have been periodic executions, the most recent in 1990. Of those arrested, only about 800 were ever brought to trial.

Assuming a basically pro-Western stance, Suharto's New Order ended confrontation with Malaysia and has since been a major promoter and participant in the regional Association of Southeast Asian Nations (ASEAN) Advised by Western-trained economists, the army-led government has encouraged direct foreign investment and received loans from the West.

Elections held in 1971 were strictly controlled, and the government organization Golkar (Joint Secretariat of Functional Groups) secured most of the seats in the largely advisory parliament. Golkar again achieved about 62 percent of the vote in the 1977 elections. Suharto was elected president by bodies emerging from both these elections.

In 1975 the state-owned oil enterprise, Pertamina, was unable to meet repayments of debts amounting to $10. 5 billion, and the crisis threatened Indonesia's financial structure. Only through project cancellations, renegotiation of loans, and help from the United States and other Western governments was Jakarta able to salvage the situation by late 1977. Subsequently, world oil prices aided Indonesia's economic recovery, and oil production and exports have increased.

A second crisis arose in the former Portuguese colony of East Timor. When Portugal withdrew from East Timor in 1975, Frente Revolucionaria do Timor Leste Independente (Fretilin), a Communist group seeking independence, held control of Dili, the capital. Indonesia considered Fretilin a threatening movement and invaded East Timor in December. Despite condemnation by Portugal and the UN, Indonesia later annexed the area as its 24th province. Human-rights organizations claim that more than 100,000 people may have been killed by the Indonesian army during the annexation. Ongoing political tensions in the region led to a massacre of pro-independence demonstrators by Indonesian soldiers in November 1991. Fighting between Indonesian troops and Fretilin members continued into the mid-1990s, despite reconciliation talks between Indonesian officials and exiled Timorese leaders.

Most opposition to the Suharto regime has come from Muslim groups that have never accepted the government's attempt to control them and from university students alienated by the regime's corruption and human-rights violations. Reacting to widespread student demonstrations in early 1978, the government tightened its control over the campuses and the press.

The greatest long-term dangers to the regime, however, were the growing social and economic inequalities, particularly the increasing landlessness among the Javanese peasantry. These inequities were exacerbated by the growth of the population, despite a relatively successful family-planning program in Java. Nevertheless, the army's aging "Generation of 1945," having monopolized power under the New Order, seemed intent on maintaining control. Golkar again won an overwhelming majority in the parliamentary elections of May 1982, and in March 1983 the parliament reelected Suharto, who ran unopposed, and broadened his presidential powers. Again running unopposed, Suharto won re-election in March 1988 and in March 1993.

Indonesia's former President Suharto turns 77 in June this year, but there will be no celebration for the man who last month surrendered his 32-year iron grip on the world's fourth most populous nation.

Forced to quit after mobs went on a rampage and angry protesters demanded he be tried for corruption, Suharto has said nothing publicly since his May 21 resignation.

222

In contrast, his successor, new President B. J. Habibie, can't seem to get enough of the limelight and is basking in the glory of rolling back many of Suharto's draconian ways.

Suharto remains holed up at his private home in Jakarta, guarded by the powerful military from growing calls for retribution against him and his super-rich family.

He rarely ventures outside the compound. Looking for solace, he recently visited a mosque. One family member said the former autocrat has slipped out to play a few rounds of golf. The aloof, king-like Suharto usually avoided the media. Habibie, meanwhile, chatted for hours Saturday with editors and foreign correspondents about his vision to bring Indonesia out of its economic crisis.

The new president has also released some political prisoners, lifted bans on labour unions and abolished restrictions on press freedoms. He has pledged to cooperate fully with the International Monetary Fund to save the economy.

Habibie has also promised new electoral reforms laws by August and the lifting of bans on the formation of new political parties. Parliamentary elections have been scheduled for next May and a 1,000-seat national assembly will chose a new president by December 1999.

Habibie's embrace of reform and reversal of Suharto's ways is a dramatic turnaround. A friend of Suharto's since the 1950s, he was rewarded for his loyalty by being elected vice-president earlier this year.

However, he denies that he is still taking orders from his former mentor. He claims not to have talked with Suharto since the former general stepped down and points to the changes he has wrought since the end of Suharto's regime. Still, Habibie appears determined to protect his old boss. Many have called for Suharto to face trial for corruption and abuse of power, and some want the state to seize billions of dollars amassed by his family. "I ask the people of the Republic of Indonesia to concentrate on the future,"

Habibie said. "It doesn't mean that corruption and nepotism and so on will be forgotten. I ask them to leave it to the legal process."

A party was held Saturday for one of Indonesia's former leaders, but it was for not Suharto. About 90 people gathered to celebrate the birth of Indonesia's founding President Sukaro.